Many People, Many Voices

Many People,
Many Voices

Poetry from the
English-speaking world

Edited by Norman Hidden
and Amy Hollins

Hutchinson of London

Hutchinson & Co. (Publishers) Ltd
3 Fitzroy Square, London W1P 6JD

London Melbourne Sydney Auckland
Wellington Johannesburg and agencies
throughout the world

First published 1978
This selection © Norman Hidden and Amy Hollins 1978

Set in IBM Century

Printed in Great Britain by the Anchor Press Ltd
and bound by Wm Brendon & Son Ltd,
both of Tiptree, Essex

British Library CIP data

Many people, many voices.
    1. English poetry — 20th century
    I. Hidden, Norman   II. Hollins, Amy
    821'.9'1208   PR1225

ISBN 0 09 133660 0 cased
ISBN 0 09 133661 9 paper

Contents

Introduction

Our People

Love

Life and Death

Animals

Nature and Seasons

Myth . . . Legend . . . The Past

Beliefs

Arts, Sports and Play

Places

Acknowledgements for Illustrations

Our People: 'The People of Odidare', woodcut by Jacob Afolabi, reproduced from *Contemporary Art in Africa* by Ulli Beier by permission of Pall Mall/Phaidon Press Ltd; photograph by Cambridge University Library

Love: ''Nave, Nave Fenua', woodcut by Paul Gauguin, reproduced from *The Art of the Print* by F. Eichenberg, Thames & Hudson Ltd, by courtesy of the Museum of Fine Arts, Boston, Massachusetts; from the W.G. Russell-Allen Bequest

Life and Death: 'Death with Child in her Lap', woodcut by Kollwitz, 1921, by courtesy of the Philadephia Museum of Art

Animals: 'The Snake', wood engraving by Robert Gibbings, 1934, reproduced by permission of Thomas Yoseloff Ltd, Photograph by Cambridge University Library

Nature: 'The Fen', woodcut by Gwen Raverat, by permission of the Fitzwilliam Museum, Cambridge

Myth . . . Legend . . . the Past: 'The sacrifice of Abraham', woodcut by Jacob Afolabi, by permission of Phaidon Press Ltd, as above

Beliefs: 'The Anti-bird Ghost', ink drawing by Twins Seven Seven, reproduced from *African Art* by Frank Willett, Thames & Hudson Ltd, by courtesy of the Edward Garrison Collection

Arts: 'The Phoenix', sculpture by the late George Fullard, reproduced by permission of Mrs Irena Fullard

Places: Caribbean Fishermen, photo by Chris Searle

Introduction

We hope that this collection of poems may suggest how much,
the world over, poets (and their readers) are concerned with
essential human values, and how much in this respect their
different cultures have to offer. These concerns — about such
values as freedom, beauty, love, honesty of purpose or, it
may be, sheer fun — come to us with fresh force when we see
not only how they are shared among so many different
peoples, but how each group of people has its own distinctive
viewpoint to contribute.

A few of the poems directly reflect the relationship
between people of different cultural backgrounds or the
'clash of cultures'. Others relate more specifically to the one
culture that the poet knows, and for whose preservation he
or she may be fighting fiercely. Still other poems are concerned with general themes, common to all peoples; and there
are one or two in which the poets display a disarming knack
of smiling at ways and customs, or an equal facility in de-
ploying dialect English to brilliant effect. Some poets employ
a linguistic style owing much to western European influences,
largely the result of their schooling and the linguistic demands
of the society they live in. Others write in a plainly un-
influenced style, but one in which spontaneity and freshness
are salient features.

Most of the poems are new, or not too old; and they are
by poets well known and not so well known. Where there
were modern translations of some of the great poems of the
past in another language, it seemed to us right to include
such translations, if only to give the merest hint that some
of the cultures represented here are much more fully alive
in their own indigenous languages.

Many of our readers, or their families, may hail from the
countries of origin of the poets here represented. The editors'
aim has been not to provide a 'Commonwealth' or a 'United
Nations' anthology, but to offer a wider than usual band of
cultural experience, that may be appreciated by all.

Our People

I am glad to be up and about

I am glad to be up and about this sunny morning,
Walking the raised path between fields,
While all around me
Are cheerful folk harvesting potatoes.

I am glad to be away from books,
Broadcasts and the familiar smells,
And the unending pursuit of a livelihood.

Small boys on their way to school
Trail their toes through the stripped soil,
And pounce with joy
Upon the marble-size potatoes left behind by the harvesters,
And with these fill their satchels.

One voice is raised in song,
While the men, hunkering on their heels,
Move up in a line like pirates
To uncover the heaps of buried treasure,
And transfer them to baskets.

And girls who should be playing with dolls
Unload the baskets into sacks
Which tonight or tomorrow night
Will be speeding in a groaning truck
To Karachi, a thousand miles away.

And this week or the following week,
Bilious businessmen and irate wives
And their washed and prattling children,
Will sit down at uncounted tables
And hastily devour the potatoes I see
With never a thought for these
Fields, these men and this sunny morning.

Taufiq Rafat, Pakistan

The song of the banana man

Touris', white man, wipin' his face,
Met me in Golden Grove market place,
He looked at m'ol' clothes brown wid stain,
An' soaked right through wid de Portlan' rain,
He cas' his eye, turn' up his nose,
He says, 'You're a beggar man, I suppose?'
He says, 'Boy, get some occupation,
Be of some value to your nation.'

I said, 'By God and dis big right han'
You mus' recognize a banana man.

'Up in de hills, where de streams are cool,
An' mullet and janga swim in de pool,
I have ten acres of mountain side,
An' a dainty-foot donkey dat I ride,
Four Gros Michel, an' four Lacatan,
Some coconut trees, and some hills of yam,
An' I pasture on dat very same lan'
Five she-goats an' a big black ram,

'Dat, by God an' dis big right han'
Is de property of a banana man.

'I leave m'yard early-morning time
An' set m'foot to de mountain climb,
I ben' m' back to de hot-sun toil,
An' m' cutlass rings on de stony soil.
Ploughin' an' weedin', diggin' an' plantin'
Till Massa Sun drop back o' John Crow mountain,
Den home again in cool evenin' time,
Perhaps whistling dis likkle rhyme,

(Sung) *'Praise God an' m' big right han'*
I will live an' die a banana man.

continued

17

'Banana day is my special day,
I cut my stems an' I'm on m' way,
Load up de donkey, leave de lan',
Head down hill to banana stan',
When de truck comes roun' I take a ride
All de way down to de harbour side —
Dat is de night, when you, touris' man,
Would change your place wid a banana man.

'Yes, by God an' m' big right han'
I will live an' die a banana man.

'De bay is calm, an' de moon is bright,
De hills look black for de sky is light,
Down at de dock is an English ship,
Restin' after her ocean trip,
While on de pier is a monstrous hustle,
Tallymen, carriers, all in a bustle,
Wid stems on deir heads in a long black snake,
Some singin' de songs dat banana men make,

'Like, (sung) *Praise God an' m' big right han'*
I will live an' die a banana man.

'Den de payment comes, an' we have some fun,
Me, Zekiel, Breda and Duppy Son.
Down at de bar near United Wharf
We knock back a white rum, bus' a laugh,
Fill de empty bag for further toil
Wid saltfish, breadfruit, coconut oil.
Den head back home to m' yard to sleep,
A proper sleep dat is long an' deep.

'Yes, by God an' m' big right han'
I will live an' die a banana man.

'So when you see dese ol' clothes brown wid stain,
An' soaked right through wid de Portlan' rain,
Don't cas' your eye nor turn your nose,

18

Don't judge a man by his patchy clothes,
I'm a strong man, a proud man, an' I'm free,
Free as dese mountains, free as dis sea,
I know myself, an' I know my ways,
An' will sing wid pride to de end o' my days

(Sung) *'Praise God an' m' big right han'*
I will live an' die a banana man.'

Evan Jones, West Indies

Lament for Barney Flanagan

(Licensee of the Hesperus Hotel)

Flanagan got up on a Saturday morning,
Pulled on his pants while the coffee was warming;
He didn't remember the doctor's warning,
   'Your heart's too big, Mr Flanagan.'

Barney Flanagan, sprung like a frog
From a wet root in an Irish bog —
May his soul escape from the tooth of the dog!
   God have mercy on Flanagan.

Barney Flanagan R.I.P.
Rode to his grave on Hennessey's
Like a bottle-cork boat in the Irish Sea.
   The bell-boy rings for Flanagan.

Barney Flanagan, ripe for a coffin,
Eighteen stone and brandy-rotten,
Patted the housemaid's velvet bottom —
   'Oh, is it you, Mr Flanagan?'

The sky was bright as a new milk token.
Bill the Bookie and Shellshock Hogan
Waited outside for the pub to open —
   'Good day, Mr Flanagan.'

At noon he was drinking in the lounge bar corner
With a sergeant of police and a racehorse owner
When the Angel of Death looked over his shoulder —
   'Could you spare a moment, Flanagan?'

Oh the deck was cut; the bets were laid;
But the very last card that Barney played
Was the Deadman's Trump, the bullet of Spades —
   'Would you like more air, Mr Flanagan?'

The priest came running but the priest came late
For Barney was banging at the Pearly Gate.
St Peter said, 'Quiet! You'll have to wait
    For a hundred masses, Flanagan.'

The regular boys and the loud accountants
Left their nips and their seven-ounces
As chickens fly when the buzzard pounces —
    'Have you heard about old Flanagan?'

Cold in the parlour Flanagan lay
Like a bride at the end of her marriage day.
The Waterside Workers' Band will play
    A brass goodbye to Flanagan.

While publicans drink their profits still,
While lawyers flock to be in at the kill,
While Aussie barmen milk the till
    We will remember Flanagan.

For Barney had a send-off and no mistake.
He died like a man for his country's sake;
And the Governor-General came to his wake.
    Drink again to Flanagan!

Despise not, O Lord, the work of Thine own hands
And let light perpetual shine upon him.

        James K. Baxter, New Zealand

Telephone conversation

The price seemed reasonable, location
Indifferent. The landlady swore she lived
Off premises. Nothing remained
But self-confession. 'Madam,' I warned,
'I hate a wasted journey — I am African.'
Silence. Silenced transmission of
Pressurized good-breeding. Voice, when it came,
Lipstick coated, long gold-rolled
Cigarette-holder pipped. Caught I was, foully.
'HOW DARK?' . . . . I had not misheard . . . . 'ARE
    YOU LIGHT
OR VERY DARK?' Button B. Button A. Stench
Of rancid breath of public hide-and-speak.
Red booth. Red pillar-box. Red double-tiered
Omnibus squelching tar. It *was* real! Shamed
By ill-mannered silence, surrender
Pushed dumbfoundment to beg simplification.
Considerate she was, varying the emphasis —
'ARE YOU DARK? OR VERY LIGHT?' Revelation came.
'You mean — like plain or milk chocolate?'
Her assent was clinical, crushing in its light
Impersonality. Rapidly, wave-length adjusted,
I chose. 'West African sepia' — and as afterthought,
'Down in my passport.' Silence for spectroscopic
Flight of fancy, till truthfulness clanged her accent
Hard on the mouthpiece. 'WHAT'S THAT?' conceding
'DON'T KNOW WHAT THAT IS.' 'Like brunette.'
'THAT'S DARK? ISN'T IT?' 'Not altogether.
Facially, I am brunette, but madam, you should see
The rest of me. Palm of my hand, soles of my feet
Are a peroxide blonde. Friction, caused —
Foolishly madam — by sitting down, has turned
My bottom raven black — One moment madam!' — sensing
Her receiver rearing on the thunderclap
About my ears — 'Madam,' I pleaded, 'wouldn't you rather
See for yourself?'

Wole Soyinka, Nigeria

The old man of Birmingham

There is no smell even in flowers; in my youth
I could get a little. I don't get even half of it.
Now the sky is pale, the grass under the foot
is half-green, the river is not blue. Besides,
the strawberry is tasteless, meat is hard
like rubber. The cows are very naughty; they give
bucketful of milk, no doubt, but not so thick.
The stupid beasts also steal easily the thickness
of their milk today. Previously here the wine is also
like water. Previously, a drink of two or three beers
would make one intoxicated, whereas now-a-days
at least five bottles at a time are necessary.

The old man of Birmingham needs them. The other day
he raised serious objection against flower,
river, grass, cloud, strawberry, meat, milk etc.,
and in the curves of his deformed face
there was not even a single drop of mercy;
inside the stomach the five bottles
of turbid beer were in action.

Nirendranath Chakrabarti, India
(translated by Pranab Bandyopadhyay)

Goodbye party for Miss Pushpa T.S.

Friends, our dear sister
is departing for foreign
in two three days,
and we are meeting today
to wish her bonnvoage.
You are all knowing, friends,
what sweetness is in Miss Pushpa,
I don't mean only external sweetness
but internal sweetness.
Miss Pushpa is smiling and smiling
even for no reason
but simply because she is feeling.
Miss Pushpa is coming
from very high family.
Her father was renowned advocate
in Bulsar or Surat,
I am not remembering now which place.
Surat? Ah, yes,
once only I stayed in Surat
with family members
of my uncle's very old friend —
his wife was cooking nicely . . .
that was long time ago.
Coming back to Miss Pushpa
she is most popular lady
with men also and ladies also.
Whenever I ask her to do anything,
she was saying, 'Just now only
I will do it.' That is showing
good spirit. I am always
appreciating the good spirit.
Pushpa Miss is never saying no,
whatever I or anybody is asking
she is always saying yes,

and today she is going
to improve her prospects
and we are wishing her bonnvoage.
Now I ask other speakers to speak
and afterwards Miss Pushpa
will do the summing up.

Nissim Ezekiel, India

Neighbour, tenth floor

Beyond a span of wall
I can imagine you:

gaping
    your sleep-soured dawnbreaths,
waking
    your habitual body,
and in a web of bedclothes
sitting up
       dishevelled
to grope for clock and eyeglasses
as I reach out for mine.

I know you pace your cage,
halfway to the sky
in this communal ivory tower,
for I hear your footsteps
echoing mine
       in the adjacent cell.

When you flush your waste
my cistern gurgles too,
and the mutter of my saucepans
answers the descant of yours.

Boxed in our hired cubicles
we act the self-same-*ings*
feeding cursing waiting
and watching television
(that disingenuous window).

We nod civilly on thresholds,
grin cosily in liftcars,
and disappear
scuttling like land-crabs
into separate occasions.

Daily I want to rush to you
weeping with recognition
and embrace you calling,
calling,
   I am your neighbour,
     Love me,

then live with you,
together away
   from these lonely dens;
but what would be the use?

It is better to tap out an endless message
against that imperceptible wall
that must always divide us.

               A. L. Hendriks, West Indies

Offal

He stooped
to pick up
offal: left-over pieces
of putrid meat and
shredded fat lying amidst
slimy intestines
and I noticed
he was old
from the withered, knotted
hands; jagged nails
scratching the insides
of the tin
that lay outside
the butcher's shop.
Use some more spice
on that
the butcher said
and give some to me
to taste.
The old man looked up
and I thought I saw
a light glow in his eyes
or was it just
the first thin film
of a tear?
But he did not
smile or cry
just walked away
holding the
offal
in his hands.

Tariq Y. Malik, Pakistan

Beggars

Life is no metaphor for them,
ideologies are copper coins
in their bowls;
your reeling traffic
is a charity show in sunlit darkness.
Their stare has the
question of the Sphinx,
emptiness gathers like
moss in their hearts.
Dreams hiccup in
dark corners of their
desolate brains and
with death-eaten fingers
sketch the bawdiness of future,
their eyes are the sinking
speculators of your
hearts' fluctuations.
Their faces speak for
the myths and legends
of your city's rise and fall.
Grace is worthy
as the coins you put into their
bowls tinkle as temple bells.

Pravin A. Parikh, India

The experiment

There he stood, through the glass, looking like us,
Blue eyes, blue shirt, suede jacket and suede shoes,
Like you or me. His head wired up, he stood
There looking normal, through the glass,
The man I killed.

'We're testing the heuristic role of pain,'
Said the Director, lying. 'He'll try and join
Two paper clips together with one hand.
You watch, you judge, you punish. If you stand
Holding this lever, pull it when he fails,
He'll get a shock, and learn. And if he fails
Again, you pull again. He fails, you pull.
He learns (or doesn't). And you watch, and pull
Again until he does. And watch the dial,
It may read DANGER.'
     So I watched and pulled.
I was the man in charge. The man I killed
Fumbled, and failed. I watched the needle quiver
Past the red line, and still I pulled the lever.

Once I turned, saying 'Are you sure? I mean — '
'Go on, please,' the Director said. 'Go on.
It is imperative the test go on.'
I pulled. He dropped the clips. I pulled. He failed.
The needle leapt; I watched the man I killed.

Later it was explained: 'We tested you,'
Said the Director. 'Most people pull the lever,
And so did you. Most people pull past DANGER,
And so did you.' And then the man I killed
Came through the door, shook hands with me, and smiled.
He didn't know how many times he'd died.
(Of course no current flowed.)

It's over now. I hated that Director
For weeks. If he'd been wired onto my lever
I would have pulled until I broke the dial,
Till his blood bubbled, brains began to boil,
— Standing there, in his scientific voice,
saying 'Go on.'
     And then when that was over,
It was myself I hated. Pulling levers,
I would wake up, and feel the shock, or see
Flesh shrivel.
     Then the man I'd killed was me.

And now that's over. What I have to carry
Now, is the knowledge that I'm ordinary.
The world is full of levers, and of us,
Who pull the levers: it's as commonplace
As glass, as people, or as burning flesh.

Laurence Lerner, South Africa

Riot area

They have burnt my hut.
Not strangers, not Police,
The people sent by Government to burn,
They have not burnt my hut,
It is my friends.
For shall I not call them friends,
That village next to ours
How cannot they be our friends
One stream gives water to us;
We mourn with them their deaths;
They cheer our weddings;
Always it has been so.
But they have burnt my hut.
One brand into the thatch
Nothing is left of my roof,
The falling timbers smashed my cups,
Chairs and tables are burnt,
A saved blanket covers me,
Now they have burnt my hut.

J.H. Chaplin, Kenya

Wooden dolls and dreams

While the drummers
Drummed
And the women
Danced
And smooth-chested men
With strong white teeth
Sang gay-sad songs
And drank palm-wine,

The swallows brought
Golden pellets of mud
To build their nests in the rafters.
They knew nothing of what the drummers
Drummed:
Nor the words the singers
Sang.
But they knew something they have always known:
That after the dance
The children will come back to the house
To play with their wooden dolls,
And the grown-ups to their dreams and visions.

Kwesi Brew, Ghana

The little chapel

When I am old and rich and gracious,
I shall have a little chapel in my garden,
And every morning I shall walk there,
Checking red roses and white.
I shall always pray in a white sari —
White is so becoming to prayer.
In the mornings I shall pray,
In the evenings pour tea.
And all the gracious ladies in the city
Will envy my tea ceremony.
And my old bones will lie comforted
With the elegance of my white sari
And my elegant porcelain.

Suniti Namjoshi, Pakistan

My busconductor

My busconductor tells me
he only has one kidney
and that may soon go on strike
through overwork.
Each busticket
takes on now a different shape
and texture.
He holds a ninepenny single
as if it were a rose
and puts the shilling in his bag
as a child into a gasmeter.
His thin lips
have no quips
for fat factorygirls
and he ignores
the drunk who snores
and the oldman who talks to himself
and gets off at the wrong stop.
He goes gently to the bedroom
of the bus
to collect
and watch familiar shops and pubs passby
(perhaps for the last time?)
The sameold streets look different now
more distinct
as through new glasses.
And the sky
was it ever so blue?

And all the time
deepdown in the deserted busshelter of his mind
he thinks about his journey nearly done.
One day he'll clock on and never clock off
or clock off and never clock on.

Roger McGough, UK

34

Baking day

Thursday was baking day in our house.
The spicy smell of new baked bread would meet
My nostrils when I came home from school and there
    would be
Fresh buns for tea, but better still were the holidays.

Then I could stay and watch the baking of the bread.
My mother would build up the fire and pull out the damper
Until the flames were flaring under the oven; while it was
    heating
She would get out her earthenware bowl and baking board.

Into the crater of flour in the bowl she would pour sugar
And yeast in hot water; to make sure the yeast was fresh
I had often been sent to fetch it from the grocer that
    morning,
And it smelt of the earth after rain as it dissolved in the
    sweet water.

Then her small stubby hands would knead and pummel
The dough until they became two clowns in baggy
    pantaloons,
And the right one, whose three fingers and blue stump
Told of the accident which followed my birth, became whole.

As the hands worked a creamy elastic ball
Took shape and covered by a white cloth was set
On a wooden chair by the fire slowly to rise:
To me the most mysterious rite of all.

From time to time I would peep at the living dough
To make sure it was not creeping out of the bowl.
Sometimes I imagined it possessed, filling the whole room,
And we helpless, unable to control its power to grow,

continued

But as it heaved above the rim of the bowl mother
Was there, taking it and moulding it into plaited loaves
And buns and giving me a bit to make into a bread man,
With currant eyes, and I, too, was a baker.

My man was baked with the loaves and I would eat him
    for tea.
On Friday night, when the plaited loaves were placed
Under a white napkin on the dining table,
Beside two lighted candles, they became holy.

No bread will ever be so full of the sun as the pieces
We were given to eat after prayers and the cutting of this
    bread.
My mother, who thought her life had been narrow, did not
    want
Her daughters to be bakers of bread. I think she was wise.

Yet sometimes, when my cultivated brain chafes at kitchen
Tasks, I remember her, patiently kneading dough
And rolling pastry, her untutored intelligence
All bent towards nourishing her children.

Rosemary Joseph, UK

Kitchens

Kitchens were places

    we grew up in.
    High-roofed, spacious,

they attracted us
with the pungency

    of smoke and spices.
    From December beds

we hurried to the cheer
of wood-fires, above

    which sang black kettles.
    Once there, we dawdled

over last night's curry
and fresh bread dripping

    from the saucepan, eggs,
    and everlasting bowls

of tea. Discussions
centred on primaries:

    births, deaths, marriages,
    crops. Mother presided

contributing only
her presence, busy

    ladling, ladling. Noise
    was warmth. Now in these

cramped spaces, there is
no time for talk. A

    stainless homogeneity
    winks back our sneers.

continued

Chairs are insular;
they do not encourage

> intimacy like slats.
> The table tucks bellies

in. We would not dream
of coming to this place

> to savour our triumphs,
> or unburden our griefs.

Chromium and formica
have replaced the textured

> homeliness of plaster, teak.
> Everything is clean

as a hospital.
The surrealist clock,

> where once the eloquent
> grandfather swung,

clicks forward, stiffly.
We are deferential

> to the snap pleasures
> of electric toast, and take

our last gulps standing up.

Taufiq Rafat, Pakistan

Love

Song for last year's wife

Alice, this is my first winter
of waking without you, of knowing
that you, dressed in familiar clothes
are elsewhere, perhaps not even
conscious of our anniversary. Have
you noticed? The earth's still as hard,
the same empty gardens exist; it is
as if nothing special had changed.
I wake with another mouth feeding
from me, yet still feel as if
Love had not the right
to walk out of me. A year now. So
what? you say. I send out my spies
to discover what you are doing. They smile,
return, tell me your body's as firm,
you are as alive, as warm and inviting
as when I knew you first . . . . Perhaps it is
the winter, its isolation from other seasons,
that sends me your ghost to witness
when I wake. Somebody came here today, asked
how you were keeping, what
you were doing. I imagine you,
waking in another city, touched
by this same hour. So ordinary
a thing as loss comes now and touches me.

Brian Patten, UK

Jarri's love song

Outside his new-made gunya Jarri
With a sudden howl started to make a song.
He had something to sing about, he
Had been given the pretty Nona,
He was making a song about Nona.
Jarri never made a song to remember
But many times he made camp laugh.
Now they laughed at Jarri's love song,
They all liked that cheerful fellow, all
But sour old Yundi.
Jarri sat with legs out
Thudding a hollow log with waddy
To make rhythm, he raised voice
To the yelling chant of the good song-men.
Nona laughed with them, proud of Jarri,
Happy to share all eyes with Jarri.
Only old Yundi scowled.
And this the love song Jarri sang them:

I got belly-bruise from a club,
But I . . . got . . . Nona!
I got a sore where I sit down
But I . . . got . . . Nona.
Lost 'em firesticks, broke it woomera,
No more fishnet, no more tomahawk,
Got no goreen, got no shield,
But I . . . got . . . Nona.

Gootchi he got bark canoe
But I . . . got . . . Nona.
Yarrawan sleep with hunting dog
But I got Nona.
Kaa got pitcheri, Gwabba got drone-pipe,
Mullawa he got three boomerangs and two dingoes,
Walla got possum-rug keep him warm,
But I . . . got . . . Nona.

continued

41

Gecko fella, he got two tails,
But I . . . got . . . Nona.
Frog he only got other frog
But I . . . got . . . Nona.
Gwoon got Weela with big hind part,
She got seven kids before he start,
Grey old Yundi got withered old Yan,
But I . . . got . . . Nona.

Kath Walker, Australia

A slice of wedding cake

Why have such scores of lovely, gifted girls
   Married impossible men?
Simple self-sacrifice may be ruled out,
   And missionary endeavour, nine times out of ten.

Repeat 'impossible men': not merely rustic,
   Foul-tempered or depraved
(Dramatic foils chosen to show the world
   How well women behave, and always have behaved).

Impossible men: idle, illiterate,
   Self-pitying, dirty, sly,
For whose appearance even in City parks
   Excuses must be made to casual passers-by.

Has God's supply of tolerable husbands
   Fallen, in fact, so low?
Or do I always over-value woman
   At the expense of man?
          Do I?
             It might be so.

Robert Graves, UK

Before the beginning

Twice the thorny bushes
leaped forward to bait her sari
as we rambled around
on the sandy river-bed,
   and each time I leaned over her
   slouched body to release the hem,
   the deep pools of her eyes held me,
   till something flickered to pother those depths again.
I arrowed a sprig into the placid
surface of the river to let it float
down to eternity,
   but before it could set out,
   a dogged whirlpool swallowed
   it under the jungle of weeds.
It's now time to roll up the picnic basket,
put away the crumbs of bread,
for she is already eye-catching a stranger
on the other side of the beach.

Shiv K. Kumar, India

43

The marriage of black and white

Marry me
And we shall have children
Who will not need sunbathing
Having been blessed with a skin
The hue that is intermediate:
True representatives
Of the race of the future:
Of the conscience that is to be
A consensus of all there is
Of culture and skins:
People who speak a language
That is universal
As the stocks from which it is derived:
The product of prides in races;
The successors over petty bigotry:
The race that will inherit
The best there is from both;
Children grown strong
Tempered by ill-knowledges
That are appendixes
In the two camps
Of colour curtains.

And Nietzsche was wrong
Against racial mixing;
He is right — if
There is no psychological homework.

My skin is so black
And potent as the coal
That the miners bring out
From the bowels of the earth,
With plenty of energy entrapped.

*

C'mon
We are not freaks,
We are of the same species
Despite the protective colouration,
Nature's own invention
For her sons' accommodations
To the various latitudes
Before the sons could conquer
Distance.

We are not freaks
I mean you are not and I am not.
And our children won't be mules —
Dead ends of crossbreedings —
On the contrary, very robust,
Best fitted to live in this their world,
A world relative and comparative,
A world shrunk by Orville and Marconi,
A world that knows no boundary,
A world in flux,
With the colour disc in full swing
Blurring the primaries,
A world betterworsened by
I-it.

Taban Lo Liyong, East Africa

Love songs

(i)

Like lightning in the clouds
She flashed away.
Her friends shadowing her
Melted in the space.
Never have I seen a girl as this:
Like patches of wild colour

continued

Her ways were playful,
Eyes abyss deep.
Round her neck swayed a string of pearls.
Enchanted bees hummed at her fragrant skin.
Revealing and hiding her beautiful form
She walked away
Arm in arm with her friends.
Smiling a glance and looting my heart
She walked away.
Moonlight exploded on her glazed finger nails.
Her fatal eyes collected massacred lovers.
I lay unconscious with wounded heart,
My ribs cut open by her stabbing glance.

Chandidas says:
It is an absorbing tale
Of an illness that does not end in the grave!

(ii)
Who was that girl?
Friend, who was that girl
Inflaming the river
With her fair skin? . . . .

The gold necklace
On the peaks of her breasts
Shone as the moon on the mountain snow.
The darkness in tears,
The shadows of the moon,
A flood of black hair rolled on her hips.
She rose from the river
Like a slice of the moon,
Glistening in twilight dark.
As I stood watching
And loosing myself,
She walked away wringing and twisting my soul
Together with her sari — dripping, blue.
My heart still shivers in a fever of love . . . .

(iii)

Like frozen lightning her fair face
I saw at the river bank,
Hair plaited as a coiled snake
Dressed with jasmin lace . . . .
Her darting glance and gentle smile
Made me eager.
Throwing and catching a ball of flowers,
She revealed in full her youthful form.
As her breasts rebelled against her dress,
Her face was bright with mischievous smiles.
And feet adorned with ankle-bells,
Were painted red.

(iv)

I have hardened my mind
Against the name of love.
Never again shall I hear of it.
If ever I do,
I shall instantly sacrifice
This miserable life.
I have no need of love.

In markets and riverbanks
Where people gather
They call me a whore,
Loading my world with terrible shame.

Yet still, shame cools my heart,
I feel his presence
Like the southern breeze
On the lotus-pool . . . .

Chandidas, India
(translated by Deben Bhattacharya)

The beloved

Lapobo,
Tall but not too tall,
Short but not too short,
She is of medium size.

Lapobo,
Her teeth are not as ash
Nor the colour of maize flour,
Her teeth are white as fresh milk.
The whiteness of her teeth
When I think of her
Makes food drop from my hand.

Lapobo,
Black but not too black,
Brown but not too brown,
Her skin colour is just between black and brown.

Lapobo,
Her heels have no cracks,
Her palms are smooth and tender to touch,
Her eyes — Ho they can destroy anybody.

A.R. Cliff-Lubwa, East Africa

Even a bishop

Do you see Elengou, Nikoles' daughter,
who's as tender as tarragon leaves?
Everyone who sees her agrees
she's lovable as snow-white bread.

48

Do you see Elengou, Nikoles' daughter?
No gold exists with which to weigh her,
no man who does not offer prayers
that she may set her mind upon him!

Do you see Elengou, Nikoles' daughter,
who's like the full moon in her power?
Both young and old are wild about her,
she entices defenceless men.

You see Elengou, Nikoles' daughter —
Watch out, my son, don't think she's fooling!
She knows the greatness of her beauty
makes even a bishop dismount.

Demetres Lipertis, Cyprus

An apology to Goutama

When other eyes haunt my thought, I kiss your
Eyes and shut them, so that I need no longer
See them brood, or their naked, naked fear.
Another voice haunts my ears, another face
My dreams, but in your arms I must today
Lie, and find an oasis where memories'
Sad winds do not so much blow, and I must
Hear you say, I love, I love, I love. It was
Another who made me lonely, not you.
Your hands with bitten nails never pain, never
Reject. Another's name brings tears, yours
A calm, and a smile, and yet, Goutama,
That other owns me; while your arms hold
My woman-form, his hurting arms
Hold my very soul.

K. Das, India

Song of the wagondriver

My first love was the ten-ton truck
they gave me when I started,
and though she played the bitch with me
I grieved when we were parted.

Since then I've had a dozen more,
the wound was quick to heal,
and now it's easier to say
I'm married to my wheel.

I've trunked it north, I've trunked it south,
on wagons good and bad,
but none were ever really like
the first I ever had.

The life is hard, the hours are long,
sometimes I cease to feel,
But I go on, for it seems to me
I'm married to my wheel.

Often I think of my home and kids,
out on the road at night,
and think of taking a local job
provided the money's right.

Two nights a week I see my wife,
and eat a decent meal,
but otherwise, for all my life,
I'm married to my wheel.

B.S. Johnson, UK

Caring for animals

I ask sometimes why these small animals
With bitter eyes, why we should care for them.

I question the sky, the serene blue water,
But it cannot say. It gives no answer.

And no answer releases in my head
A procession of grey shades patched and whimpering,

Dogs with clipped ears, wheezing cart horses,
A fly without shadow and without thought.

Is it with these menaces to our vision,
With this procession led by a man carrying wood

We must be concerned? The holy land, the rearing
Green island should be kindlier than this.

Yet the animals, our ghosts, need tending to.
Take in the whipped cat and the blinded owl;

Take up the man-trapped squirrel upon your shoulder.
Attend to the unnecessary beasts.

From growing mercy and a moderate love
Great love for the human animal occurs.

And your love grows. Your great love grows and grows.

Jon Silkin, UK

To an outstanding failure

Who will remember you when I have gone?
   Who will listen for you?
Then you exchange your shaky reputation
   for oblivion,
for blank looks on the readers' faces,
for no sadness at the foot of tombstones.

If I record your more than jaunty step,
   your thin arms cradling fruit
at knock-down bargain prices, eyes swimming
   with hypnotic booze
and misty recognition, how remarkable
is that? Not enough to raise the flicker

of an interest. Joseph Samuel Evans . . .
   apathetic Mason
who rarely paid the dues, declined to climb
   to order; mystery boy
beloved of your uncle; pianist
extraordinary; quiet man

and kind. You liked your thinning hair combed
   gently after supper.
You liked a cheap and clean cherrywood,
   with execrable twist.
You loved to talk about your infants, and
you wept like one the day my brother died.

A man of wit, of taste, of many gifts
   all nicely drowned in drink.
Nothing of your artistry remains,
   other than a sample
of commercial scumble, some odd pickings
from the saleroom and the family hands.

Amy Hollins, UK

Life and Death

The birth of Shaka
(born illegitimate)

a light appeared in the bush
the nearby trees were confounded
branches and leaves gathered

he was a few minutes old

only the winds knew his name
shouting loud through the leaves
and an army of bees passing by
hummed a call of salute

He opened his mouth and cried
gave no explanation of grieved
tears going down his mother's breast

a mouse walked by tactfully
coming close to find out
such a strange new cry
from the bush at dawn

Khadambi Asalache, Kenya

Not waving but drowning

Nobody heard him, the dead man,
But still he lay moaning:
I was much further out than you thought
And not waving but drowning.

Poor chap, he always loved larking
And now he's dead
It must have been too cold for him his heart gave way,
They said.

Oh, no no no, it was too cold always
(Still the dead one lay moaning)
I was much too far out all my life
And not waving but drowning.

Stevie Smith, UK

A country death

And when her husband died, of course she went
to live in the country with her married
daughter; there the air and food sustained her
well enough, but she missed the London streets.

Her son-in-law was — not rich exactly,
but — he had to spare, and knew of fallow
places where lamp-posts went when finished with,
knew what they did with them when they were old.

So, incongruous amongst the Sussex elms,
the lamp-post came and stood before the house,
a London exile itself; alight at
dusk, it was to make her feel less homesick.

All credit to the giver; but still this
old woman's life was fretful, and her death
had nothing of the peace for which they hoped:
what do you do with them when they are old?

B.S. Johnson, UK

Requiem for a Caribbean fisherman

Raking long furrows with his little boat's prow
Gathering small harvests with his scything net,
All his time he farmed acres of the sea.

By nature as by circumstance solitary,
He knew no hollowness in his shallow dug-out
Considering pathways of the fish, and of clouds and stars.
Learning the geometry of waters and the verse of weathers.

By reason of strength he lived fourscore years
And by *braata* of *Big-Massa* yet another seven.
He died uncomplaining after saying he was sleepy.

To catalogue his virtues and relegate his failures
Can avail him nothing, nor much avail us.

What we can do for him ultimately now
Is rest him calm in the narrowest of craft,
Point him desolately toward the horizon.

A.L. Hendriks, West Indies

To the Indians who died in Africa

A man's destination is his own village,
His own fire, and his wife's cooking;
To sit in front of his own door at sunset
And see his grandson, and his neighbour's grandson
    Playing in the dust together.

Scarred but secure, he has many memories
Which return at the hour of conversation,
(The warm or the cool hour, according to the climate)
Of foreign men, who fought in foreign places,
    Foreign to each other.

A man's destination is not his destiny,
Every country is home to one man
And exile to another. Where a man dies bravely
At one with his destiny, that soil is his.
  Let his village remember.

This was not your land, or ours: but a village in the Midlands,
And one in the Five Rivers, may have the same graveyard.
Let those who go home tell the same story of you:

Of action with a common purpose, action
None the less fruitful if neither you nor we
Know, until the judgment after death,
  What is the fruit of action.

T.S. Eliot, UK

An un-African breakfast
(spoken to a free guitar accompaniment)

So here I am this morning
Early in the kitchen.

The aroma of fresh coffee on the boil,
  Nose-filling aroma of good fresh coffee
    on the boil;
  And this kitchen is good to be in
  And good to hear the browning water
    babble-bubbling inside the glass-trap
    head of the percolator;
And the good wife still asleep in her vono bed
Dreaming good dreams, I hope,
Of me!

All night the tummy hasn't been well,
   Running like it wanted nothing more
      to do with me for eating what I
      do not know —
   All night a running tummy;
   Till at last out of weariness
   I drop into oblivion between 4 and 5
   Quite unknowing —
      Deep oblivion
      Sweet as feathers . . . .

Then crash out of nowhere
The white day comes bursting in
   Through frosted louvres . . . .

And it's good to be alive!

Good indeed to be alive,
   So thank we god
   For everything,
      And the myriad sparrows
      Chirruping in the fresh morning sun outside
      While the percolator bubbles.

And here a loaf of bread
And there a jar of marmalade
And sugar for the dreaming wife
And milk just turned out of its blue tin
   now rolling
   on its back
   like a cat,
And there the frying-pan on the gas cooker
   And two eggs spluttering away —
   Yolk of golden egg with garnishing of
      onion and new-cut pepper green and
      winking red,
And a little salt
   A little salt . . . .

Oh damn!
A hot speck of spitting oil near got me
In the eye.

Yes reader
What d'you say?

Oh, mustn't I?
   Mustn't drink good coffee in the
      morning,
   Mustn't eat good bread and marmalade
     for breakfast,
   Mustn't fry eggs over a gas cooker
     While my good wife
     Still lies dreaming,
And mustn't read books, I suppose,
Nor write poetry,
   Because —
What d'you say?
   Because
   Not African!

But listen
The radio in my sitting-room
(I should have told you of the radio):
Listen —
   Drum sounds on *15 megacycles*
   signalling the new day in Africa,
   Pop sounds
   Calling the waking continent
   To the Breakfast Show,
   Many-tongued voices
Daring all men everywhere
     To breathe in the dawn-fresh winds
     Blowing across a changing world.

And the warrior chieftains pass on
And the beaded maidens dance away
And we sit by the running waters
   And sigh for an innocence that is gone.

But here —
    The eggs are done;

And still it's good to be alive!

And though I cannot whistle out loud
I know there is joy
    Bubbling like coffee inside me,
Sweet aromatic joy
    Of being alive,
        So thank we god
            For everything
            And the myriad sparrows
            Chirruping in the fresh morning sun outside
            While the percolator babbles,
And I feel coming alive within me
The first movement of an un-African poem.

Joe de Graft, Ghana

Another old man

On my ancestor's tomb
this epitaph's cut:
HE WAS UPRIGHT, MODEST, AND AFFABLE.
That's possible, but
let my epitaph say:

SOMETIMES THINKING ALOUD
HE WENT HIS OWN WAY.
HE WAS JOKY BY NATURE,
SAD, SCEPTICAL, PROUD.
WHAT HE NEVER WOULD FOLLOW,
OR LEAD, WAS A CROWD.

William Plomer, UK

Life

I do not want to die in this beautiful world,
But live in the hearts of men,
And find a niche in the sun-sprinkled, flowered forest.
The play of life heaves like waves
With its tears and smiles,
Meeting and parting!
Stringing together
Man's joys and sorrows,
I want to build on this earth
My eternal home.
Ever new flower-songs I bring to blossom,
For you to gather them, dawn and dusk.
Take them smiling —
And alas, when they wither
Scatter them far away.

Rabindranath Tagore, India
(translated by Aurobindo Bose)

Fruit

Now with the threat growing still greater within me,
    The Church dead that was hopelessly over-restored,
The fruit picked from these yellowing Worcestershire orchards
    What is left to me, Lord?

To wait until next year's bloom at the end of the garden
    Foams to the Malvern Hills, like an inland sea,
And to know that its fruit, dropping in autumn stillness,
    May have outlived me.

John Betjeman, UK

61

Do the dying cry?

The balcony shakes, the wrought-iron bars
melt as she cries, holding them,
I holding my father's hand
down in the street, looking up, seeing her
mouth swallow her face, and behind her
a silent room. Behind the balcony
with wrought-iron bars.
She's dying. Probably she's dead, my father
says, tries to walk away. I cannot ask
who is dying, who is probably dead.

The carob tree begins to move where the leaves
are freest. One leaf touches the balcony;
and from the hill a dog's barking
imitates her dying-cry — the wind carries
both to the sea, drops them there,
returns to the balcony, to me under it,
holding my father's hand with a question:

Do the dying cry on balconies, do they resent
this sudden misplacement? — Come, now,
you are old enough to know: her *mother* must be
dead, behind that balcony, in that silent room.

Taner Baybars, Cyprus

Animals

The jaguar

The apes yawn and adore their fleas in the sun.
The parrots shriek as if they were on fire, or strut
Like cheap tarts to attract the stroller with the nut.
Fatigued with indolence, tiger and lion

Lie still as the sun. The boa-constrictor's coil
Is a fossil. Cage after cage seems empty, or
Stinks of sleepers from the breathing straw.
It might be painted on a nursery wall.

But who runs like the rest past these arrives
At a cage where the crowd stands, stares, mesmerized,
As a child at a dream, at a jaguar hurrying enraged
Through prison darkness after the drills of his eyes

On a short fierce fuse. Not in boredom —
The eye satisfied to be blind in fire,
By the bang of blood in the brain deaf the ear —
He spins from the bars, but there's no cage to him

More than to the visionary his cell:
His stride is wildernesses of freedom:
The world rolls under the long thrust of his heel.
Over the cage floor the horizons come.

Ted Hughes, UK

Night of the scorpion

I remember the night my mother
was stung by a scorpion. Ten hours
of steady rain had driven him
to crawl beneath a sack of rice.
Parting with his poison — flash
of diabolic tail in the dark room —
he risked the rain again.
The peasants came like swarms of flies
and buzzed the Name of God a hundred times
to paralyse the Evil One.
With candles and with lanterns
throwing giant scorpion shadows
on the mud-baked walls
they searched for him: he was not found.
They clicked their tongues.
With every movement that the scorpion made
his poison moved in Mother's blood, they said.

May he sit still, they said.
May the sins of your previous birth
be burned away tonight, they said.
May your suffering decrease
the misfortunes of your next birth, they said.
May the sum of evil
balanced in this unreal world
against the sum of good
become diminished by your pain.
May the poison purify your flesh
of desire, and your spirit of ambition,
they said, and they sat around
on the floor with my mother in the centre,
the peace of understanding on each face.

More candles, more lanterns, more neighbours,
more insects, and the endless rain.
My mother twisted through and through
groaning on a mat.

continued

My father, sceptic, rationalist,
trying every curse and blessing,
powder, mixture, herb and hybrid.
He even poured a little paraffin
upon the bitten toe and put a match to it.
I watched the flame feeding on my mother.
I watched the holy man perform his rites
to tame the poison with an incantation.
After twenty hours
it lost its sting.

My mother only said
Thank God the scorpion picked on me
and spared my children.

Nissim Ezekiel, India

We all have our superstitions

We all have our superstitions
mine are snakes
no instinct-fear
of flashing eye and coil
nor is my past
mined with lariat-traumas
of the umbilical cord;
but a fear almost rational
for after each serpent-dawn
disaster struck
news of sickness, news of death
and near at home once after he appeared
a dehydrating baby
inching towards delirium

Then on the fifth night of *shrawan*
(when Garur, the eagle-god
is said to sweat with fear)
and we, like others
had made a *Shreshnag*
from lashed blades of straw
and offered it milk in an earthen bowl
and parched grain, the hind legs
of our dog Tiger
froze paralytic.
His lungs strained and heaved
like a pair of bellows — and broke.
Pointing out the purple tongue
the Vet, who only a minute ago
had treated him for colic, said
'Sure as death, he died of snake-bite.'

K.N. Daruwalla, India

Army ants

(The army ants not only make their houses but they are their house, for
of their own living bodies they form the whole complicated dwelling.
C. Judson Herrick, *The Thinking Machine*)

Ancestors give them aristocratic tastes:
separate apartments
for the queen,
colonies

for the various castes,
several nurseries
for the abstract

and the bean-eyed young,
hung perhaps with tigerheads
of red wild ants

for trophies, or for vitamins.

Army ants build each builder
for a brick, altar
and martyr in one,

or a tile on the floor,
part of the prize decor
for the bedroom

of their most illustrious queen
where slow males
die young

or live older than death in nurseries of eggs.

Extremists, true makers
of made things, they have
only themselves

for bricks; knees for hinges; heads
for the plinths of their rain-
soaked Corinths;

the rafter a chainmail of stares
and the running
runway

a crazy pavement of hands and feet.

Not like the Great Wall of China
cemented with slave
and enemy

and the favourite almost dead;
the living, the young
are the brick

and the mortar of this house
without legend.
And the work,

as they say, is the workman at last.

A.K. Ramanujan, India

Peacock

Moving slow and gorgeous
as in the feathered radiance
of a dream
and without defence
as Beauty and Delight
always have been,
he's the poet among birds

Only in a cage
where he can strut and astound
is he secure
from claws and fangs
indifferent
to the elegant loveliness
of his elongated vulnerable tail

Pride-besotted creature
to have so many eyes
and to be so blind

Irving Layton, Canada

Turkeys observed

One observes them, one expects them;
Blue-breasted in their indifferent mortuary,
Beached bare on the cold marble slabs
In immodest underwear frills of feather.

The red sides of beef retain
Some of the smelly majesty of living:
A half-cow slung from a hook maintains
That blood and flesh are not ignored.

But a turkey cowers in death.
Pull his neck, pluck him, and look —
He is just another poor forked thing,
A skin bag plumped with inky putty.

He once complained extravagantly
In an overture of gobbles;
He lorded it on the claw-flecked mud
With a grey flick of his Confucian eye.

Now, as I pass the bleak Christmas dazzle,
I find him ranged with his cold squadrons:
The fuselage is bare, the proud wings snapped,
The tail-fan stripped down to a shameful rudder.

Seamus Heaney, UK

The world of the wash basin spider

The Wash Basin Spider's life is spent
In a slippery white enamel world
Of scented landmarks:
Shaving-brush shade tree,
Safety razor cannon,
Toothpaste tube and toothbrush road-blocks,
Stonehenge bars of soap,
One for the sunrise basin
And one for the Druidic bath.

Then there are the underground horrors,
Coming round the bend:
Knocking noises,
Tappet-knocks,
Half-hearted gushes,
Vicious spurts.

But the Spider's miniature Atlantic,
Rubber plugged, hot or cold,
Is as final as rain: with the Sargasso
Waiting down the drain.

Andrew Salkey, West Indies

Keep off the grass

The grass is a green mat
trimmed with gladioli
red like flames in a furnace.
The park bench, hallowed,
holds the loiterer listening
to the chant of the fountain
showering holy water on a congregation
of pigeons.

Keep off the grass,
Dogs not under leash forbidden.

Then madam walks her Pekinese,
Bathed and powdered and perfumed.
He sniffs at the face of the 'Keep Off' sign
with a nose as cold as frozen fish
and salutes it with a hind paw
leaving it weeping in anger and shame.

Oswald Mbuyiseni Mtshali, South Africa

Feeding ducks

One duck stood on my toes.
The others made watery rushes after bread
Thrown by my momentary hand; instead,
She stood duck-still and got far more than those.

An invisible drone boomed by
With a beetle in it; the neighbour's yearning bull
Bugled across five fields. And an evening full
Of other evenings quietly began to die.

And my everlasting hand
Dropped on my hypocrite duck her grace of bread.
And I thought, 'The first to be fattened, the first to be dead,'
Till my gestures enlarged, wide over the darkening land.

Norman MacCaig, UK

The hunt

That day the doe was killed,
I saw them coming slowly
Against a sky that was dim,
Colourless, and their faces blurred.
Outside, the fires were lit and flaming.
Voices like flies, suddenly turned bees,
Gathering up the sounds around them.
They came in slowly and put her down,
Hushed voices and loving hands lifted her,
Beside her, the fawn rested content.
They gave her looks like a lover,
Caressed her smooth loins tenderly,
And then suddenly left her, to others.
Then they stripped, hacked and cut,
And put aside the sorrow in her eyes.

That day my child cried with doe eyes
And the food on the plate was warm ash.

Ira De, India

Dichloro-diphenyl-trichloro-ethane
(DDT)

When man with his chemical sprays
has killed off the weeds
and in the fields poppies drop
their dried blood
the Queen Anne's lace lies withered —
butterflies also expire

74

those with wings half white, half orange:
the red admirals, the painted ladies —
and the little cornflower blues
who hug the hard dry soil
like blue sailed yachts that stay
a horizon's wave from the shore

not to mention the more mundane cabbage
whites and brimstone yellows —
when man has killed off all these
and their gorgeous cousins
and splendid relations
in the jungle

then an inventor will ingeniously construct
and manufacturers will produce
little plastic transistorised apparatuses
buzzing quietly through the lower air
released in their thousands
by the Arts Council —
in each municipal park
swerving, swooping, and (by regulation)
fitted with silencers:

these mechanical sylphs
will become all the rage
obtainable in boutiques
sold by the score in Carnaby Street
will replace balloons on New Year's Eve
then, suddenly
will be discarded with other
last year's fashions.

and that which killed the butterflies
will rot our bones slowly
powdering the world to one dead grey.

Norman Hidden, UK

I saw a jolly hunter

I saw a jolly hunter
  With a jolly gun
Walking in the country
  In the jolly sun.

In the jolly meadow
  Sat a jolly hare.
Saw the jolly hunter.
  Took jolly care.

Hunter jolly eager —
  Sight of jolly prey.
Forgot gun pointing
  Wrong jolly way.

Jolly hunter jolly head
  Over heels gone.
Jolly old safety-catch
  Not jolly on.

Bang went the jolly gun.
  Hunter jolly dead.
Jolly hare got clean away.
  Jolly good, I said.

R.I.J.P.

Charles Causley, UK

76

Nature and Seasons

Nature

We have neither Summer nor Winter,
Neither Autumn nor Spring.

We have instead the days
When gold sun shines on the lush green canefields —
Magnificently.

The days when the rain beats like bullets on the roofs
And there is no sound but the swish of water in the
    gullies
And trees struggling in the high Jamaica winds.

Also there are the days when the leaves fade from off
    guango trees
And the reaped canefields lie bare and fallow in the
    sun.

But best of all there are the days when the mango
    and the logwood blossom.

When the bushes are full of the sound of bees and
    the scent of honey,
When the tall grass sways and shivers to the slightest
    breath of air,

When the buttercups have paved the earth with
    yellow stars,
And beauty comes suddenly and the rains have gone.

H.D. Carberry, West Indies

Watermelon breakfast

Green rind,
dark pink flesh glistening
grainy trail
on your face as if
you gave up washing lipstick
halfway.
And the pips
the pips should be mentioned,
the way they speckle the fruit
are left stranded
boats without masts
when their red ocean
slides down the throat.
New they shine on the plate:
if we left them long enough,
they'd harden.

Take thread
exchange them for balding chickens
on a hot day
ochre ground
hard as bare feet
the dust lifting
the flies falling
a sharp smell of sweat,
and there, far away, the hills
faint as green rinds
deliquescent
the sea, the Indian ocean.
If you look hard,
how the sharks rip that blue
apart. If they were large
or not stunned by the day,
you would see the water
fall apart in chunks

continued

and the sharks
neat in their shells, black
watermelon pips.

And what about the chickens?
The kraal, the sharks, the ocean?
Surely this leads somewhere?

The chickens? Stringy.
The kraal? Bulldozed.
The houses pus on the hills.
But the ocean is learning ways
to stick together.
That's another country.
They eat the rinds there, down to the quick.

The watermelon, back to the watermelon.
Now all that sweet pulp's gone
except for the trail on your chin.
All that's left are two green cuticles
thirty black pips.
We'll string them together in amulets
to ward off the ghosts
and start again, sharing
the vast, arced smile
of wet watermelons.

Robert Greig, South Africa

Hibiscus

I see her walking in her garden in the morning;
    Her feet follow her eyes
            to where hibiscus grows.
Her hair falls like the night behind her.

Observant and aware
               she throws
The wind about her shoulders;
Assured of bloom, most certain of the way.
    Her fingers clasp the stem and pluck the sun.

She wears her flower like a golden day.

Barbara Ferland, West Indies

Poinsettias

Near cabbages
        cucumbers
        duck's eggs
        fresh
        and stale —
A miracle!
Poinsettias
        this morning
        for sale!

Sunburst wasn't enough.
Dark poinsettias
Lay in the throbbing wombs of life
Before creation was.

Don't wear them in hair!
That's not delicate.
Tongues lolling in the dark,
They sweep like fate.

But generally, like sentinels
        In bowls of nervous peace
They whisper their soft catspaw hymns
        When the words of night cease.

P. Lal, India

Rain

drops and showers of rain
washing this dirty and dry town,
birds hopelessly flying to wet shelters
roads becoming wet and grey
coloured objects bearing clearer colours
platoons of raindrops play about
on the schoolyard
trees whispering to one another saying
'what a lovely day for growing'
vehicles overtaking one another
splashing jets of water all around
the naked flagpost,
labourers go home wet and fresh
and this curtain of rain
obstructs the vision of drivers
and cyclists wearing glasses

the sun is having a short vacation, happy
like a teacher with a surprise-holiday,
coming out soon after losing its patience
while motorcyclists bow and shudder
bearing in mind the dangerously slippery road

a bus passes by
followed by the shunting of a japanese train
emitting steamed-diesel to the cold sky
heavy lorries chase wetness from their murderous wheels
1967 rain has arrived
wetting everyone and everything equally,
my bones affected by it
as bones of bending farmers get cold while
planting padi depending so much on rain,
they thank God for their rain
they with their own fondness
we with our own hatred
of the rainy season
that turns grey trouser legs reddish brown
cooling umbrella tops

walking in the rain unprotected
releases good appetite

the subdued sun began to show its anger
by appearing on the wet schoolyard

Omar Mohd. Noor, Malaysia

from   Hurricane

I remember the night,
black with slack rain,
flaccid when it first began
but with brick drops beating later on
like jump-Poco drumthumps,
beating back the coming morning,
beating with purpose,
routine, rhythm and ritual,
beating like the bounce of batter hide,
hide battered on a shoemaker's block,
batter hide, hide battered,
pane shatter, shattered pane,
batter hide, pane shatter through to dawn.

One bad, sneakin' breeze-blow
take time an' creep up
'pon Joe-Joe life
an' tear him shirt-tail
like bud-feather,
bruck him one-room in two
like chew-stick,
kill him common law wife,
kill him fait'ful goat
kill him layin'-hen then,
an' go 'way sof', sof' like tief,
like it wasn't causin' no bodders
inside the lan', at all, at all.

Andrew Salkey, West Indies

Myth . . . Legend
. . . The Past

The huntsman

Kagwa hunted the lion,
    Through bush and forest went his spear.
One day he found the skull of a man
    And said to it, 'How did you come here?'
The skull opened its mouth and said
    'Talking brought me here.'

Kagwa hurried home;
    Went to the king's chair and spoke:
'In the forest I found a talking skull.'
    The king was silent. Then he said slowly
'Never since I was born of my mother
    Have I seen or heard of a skull which spoke.'

The king called out his guards:
    'Two of you now go with him
And find this talking skull;
    But if his tale is a lie
And the skull speaks no word,
    This Kagwa himself must die.'

They rode into the forest;
    For days and nights they found nothing
At last they saw the skull; Kagwa
    Said to it 'How did you come here?'
The skull said nothing. Kagwa implored,
    But the skull said nothing.

The guards said 'Kneel down.'
    They killed him with sword and spear.
Then the skull opened its mouth;
    'Huntsman, how did you come here?'
And the dead man answered
    'Talking brought me here.'

Edward Lowbury, UK

The Fulani creation story

At the beginning there was a huge drop of milk.
Then Doondari came and he created the stone.
Then the stone created iron;
And iron created fire;
And fire created water;
And water created air.
Then Doondari descended the second time.
And he took the five elements
And he shaped them into man.
But man was proud.
Then Doondari created blindness, and blindness defeated man.
But when blindness became too proud,
Doondari created sleep, and sleep defeated blindness;
But when sleep became too proud,
Doondari created worry, and worry defeated sleep;
But when worry became too proud,
Doondari created death, and death defeated worry.
But then death became too proud,
Doondari descended for the third time,
And he came as Gueno, the eternal one.
And Gueno defeated death.

Wole Soyinka, Nigeria

A speculation

(There is a small town in the Punjab whose name means, literally, 'Village of the Assassins')

This is a mud-infested town
Lost in a blaze of sun throughout the day,
Untroubled by a road, surrounded
By a quiet profusion of fields
Defiant with stake-high corn.

The women work the fields,
Anklet-burdened, stooping to the grain
Or swaying hungrily to the single well:
The water deep, receding from the light.

No children play in the refuse of the lanes,
No voices stir the silent, dragging day;
The air is left
To the warm drone of flies, to the soft plod
Of buffaloes, imposing on the dust.

The houses stoop together at one end,
Sackcloth and straw fall at the entrances;
The smoke works, timid and concentric
Within each courtyard, and the beetles click
In the shaking, rotten beams.

There is an absence and a memory here
Soaked into the deep ink-red
Scattered across the walls, speaking from the scars
Grown dark and age-locked in the green trunks
Of the bending, growing trees.

And at night, when the moon abstains,
The men file, white and silent, on the path:
Hurry, intent and silent, and silently
Return just as the town
Surrenders peace before the growing sun.

Then the women return to the grain,
Bending and scything in a busy arc,
Lost in their work, creating
A rhythm and a pause, until one night,
One moonless, manless and remembered night
Across the treacherous, resuming river
And past the high corn the avengers come.

Shahid Hosain, Pakistan

Ancestral faces

They sneaked into the limbo of time,
But could not muffle
The gay jingling bells on
The frothy necks of sacrificial sheep
That limped and nodded after them.
They could not hide the moss on the bald pate
Of their reverend heads,
And the gnarled barks of the *wawa* tree;
Nor the rust on the ancient state-swords,
Nor the skulls studded with grinning cowries.
They could not silence the drums,
The fibre of their souls and ours —
The drums that whisper to us behind black sinewy hands,
They gazed and
Sweeping like white locusts through the forests
Saw the same men, slightly wizened,
Shuffle their sandalled feet to the same rhythms,
They heard the same words of wisdom uttered
Between puffs of pale blue smoke.
They saw us,
And said: *They have not changed*!

Kwesi Brew, Ghana

The pond

There was this pond in the village
and little boys, he heard till he was sick,
were not allowed too near;
Unfathomable pool, they said,
that swallowed men and animals just so;
and in its depths, old people said,
swam galliwasps and nameless horrors;
bright boys kept away.

Though drawn so hard by prohibitions,
the small boy, fixed in fear, kept off;
till one wet summer, grass growing lush,
paths muddy, slippery, he found himself
there at the fabled edge.

The brooding pond was dark.
Sudden, escaping cloud, the sun
came bright; and, shimmering in guilt,
he saw his own face peering from the pool.

Mervyn Morris, West Indies

Three songs of war

I

He leads his men towards the bend of
    the Acaa River,

He leads his men towards the bend of
    the Acaa River,
Morongole, the host of Piromoi,
Moves towards the bend of the River

Oh, yes, at Lumorogelo,
Our spears will clash at Lumorogelo;
Ee, he leads his men towards the final
    assault;
Morongole, the host of Piromoi
Will slaughter men at the bend of the
    Acaa River;
Oh, yes, at Lumorogelo,
Our spears will clash at Lumorogelo.

II

The place was awful,

The place was awful,
Men perished in the bamboo forest;
The place was awful,
Men perished in the bamboo forest;
Men were slaughtered in the bamboo
    forest,
The warriors of Piribong were finished,
And Piribong was left in the dust;
Lumoi, listen to the drumming footsteps
Of the escaping warriors; Agola
    Lumoi,
The place was awful.

III

The host of Palaro,
    only a few, you can count them,

The host of Palaro,
    only a few, you can count them,
Lifted the sky from its base;
Ee, the Lango fled;
They lifted the sky from its base

continued

The host of Palaro,
    only a few, you can count them,
Shook the mountain of the Lango,
Ee, the Lango wailed;
They lifted the sky from its base.

Okot p'Bitek, East Africa

Skirmish at Maldon
(a.d. 993)

I

Brilliant the sea-ripples, shining the byrnies.
Shields glint golden, tight-gripped.
The sweat of noonday glistens.

II

Now night swoops its black eagle, dead
Eyes stare starwards, and from them
Mud oozes along the tide-flats of Maldon.

Norman Hidden, UK

Beliefs

There is one God

1

There is one God.
His name is Truth.
He is the creator,
He is without fear or hate.
He is beyond time immortal,
His spirit pervades the universe.
He is not born,
Nor does He die to be reborn,
He is self-existent.
By *Guru's* grace shalt thou worship Him.

2

Never forget Him
    by whose grace thou art a noble creation.
Sing His glory, Nanak,
    by whose grace thou art honoured.

3

His praises are endless,
    endless are words of His glory,
His deeds are endless,
    endless are His gifts.
His vision is endless.
    endless is His power,
His purpose is endless,
    endless is His realisation.

4

The fools are those
   who eat and drink
      but don't think of the Giver,
and those who suffer
   from hunger, pain and misery
      are also the gifts of Lord.

5

He is the creator of the universe.
   He shall remain
      even if the worlds be ruined;
The King of Kings,
   the supreme Lord He is,
O Nanak, we abide by His will.

Guru Nanak, India
(translated by Pranap Bandyapadhyay)

from *Getting to know fish*

Being a good Mohammedan, father said:
'Friday is the day to pray and throw bread
to the fish.' In Sialkot was a river,

and I in my sailor suit four years old
walked to it holding my father's finger:
we had flour mother had kneaded and rolled
into balls, and scraps of food grown green with mould.

From the bridge I aimed at fish, my moth-balls
of flour changing shapes — first as shells
humming in the air, then like grated cheese
settling on the water as on a dish.
The fish came and swallowed, the water creased
with waves and father said: 'Let's go pray and wish
for goodness now that we have fed the fish.'

The mosque had a goldfish pond with tiny
fish — as good a proof of God as any.
I never prayed. The Arabic was too
subtle and I'd only blow bubbles through my teeth.
I sat by the pond (a foot stuck into
the water, kicking fish when the old priest
wasn't looking) and felt heaven with my feet.

Zulfikar Ghose, Pakistan

Stones

They pound prayer
against this Wall
and the dust of uttered word
settles in its crevices.

96

They lay on gentle
hands in benediction
and the fire of faith
kindles to the touch.

Our history is stone's
heaped-up affirmations

Abraham binding God
on votive altar

Jacob's laddered heaven
dreamed out of pillowed stone

despair of prophet's
broken tablets

Joshua's tribal twelve
at Jordan's bank

David's kingship springing
out of well-aimed sling

sanctuaries of stone unhewn,
built, rebuilt, destroyed . . .

the huddled headstones
of many days
gathering faith
in the faceless grief of exile.

And now this Wall,
survivor of our survival,
backing on God's ruined house
rooted in Jewish time
bearing tidings of a return

the shattered tablets
reach out for a mending hand.

Chaim Lewis, South Africa

Worship of the Buddha

The drums of war resound.
The soldiers want to gather for *Jama*, the King of Death.
Their battle-dress terrifies,
They clench their teeth!
Restless with the heat of cruelty,
They seek His blessing
Who is the sea of Infinite Mercy.
Therefore, defiantly
They march to *Buddha's* temple.
Trumpet and kettledrum pound with rage!
The earth trembles in fear!

Shouting, they pray:
May cries of anguish echo among the houses
Breaking human bonds!
May villages be charred to ashes,
And homes of learning ruined
By the sky's flaming rain!
For this, they proudly pray
To *Buddha*, the Merciful.
Trumpet and kettledrum pound with rage!
The earth trembles in fear!

To the rhythm of the victory-drum
The dead shall be counted:
Torn bodies of women and children
Shall rouse hilarious dancing.
And all breath be stopped by
The flying poison of the air,
With raised fists they march,
To make *Buddha* one of them.
Trumpet and kettledrum pound with rage!
The earth trembles in fear.

Rabindranath Tagore, India
(translated by Aurobindo Bose)

98

Church going

Once I am sure there's nothing going on
I step inside, letting the door thud shut.
Another church: matting, seats, and stone,
And little books; sprawlings of flowers, cut
For Sunday, brownish now; some brass and stuff
Up at the holy end; the small neat organ;
And a tense, musty, unignorable silence,
Brewed God knows how long. Hatless, I take off
My cycle-clips in awkward reverence,

Move forward, run my hand around the font.
From where I stand, the roof looks almost new —
Cleaned, or restored? Someone would know: I don't.
Mounting the lectern, I peruse a few
Hectoring large-scale verses, and pronounce
'Here endeth' much more loudly than I'd meant.
The echoes snigger briefly. Back at the door
I sign the book, donate an Irish sixpence,
Reflect the place was not worth stopping for.

Yet stop I did: in fact I often do,
And always end much at a loss like this,
Wondering what to look for, wondering, too,
When churches fall completely out of use
What we shall turn them into, if we shall keep
A few cathedrals chronically on show,
Their parchment, plate and pyx in locked cases,
And let the rest rent-free to rain and sheep.
Shall we avoid them as unlucky places?

Or, after dark, will dubious women come
To make their children touch a particular stone;
Pick simples for a cancer; or on some
Advised night see walking a dead one?
Power of some sort or other will go on
In games, in riddles, seemingly at random;

continued

99

But superstition, like belief, must die,
And what remains when disbelief has gone?
Grass, weedy pavement, brambles, buttress, sky,

A shape less recognisable each week,
A purpose more obscure. I wonder who
Will be the last, the very last, to seek
This place for what it was; one of the crew
That tap and jot and know what rood-lofts were?
Some ruin-bibber, randy for antique,
Or Christmas-addict, counting on a whiff
Of gown-and-bands and organ-pipes and myrrh?
Or will he be my representative,

Bored, uninformed, knowing the ghostly silt
Dispersed, yet tending to this cross of ground
Through suburb scrub because it held unspilt
So long and equably what since is found
Only in separation — marriage, and birth,
And death, and thoughts of these — for whom was built
This special shell? For, though I've no idea
What this accoutred frowsty barn is worth,
It pleases me to stand in silence here;

A serious house on serious earth it is,
In whose blent air all our compulsions meet,
Are recognised, and robed as destinies.
And that much never can be obsolete,
Since someone will forever be surprising
A hunger in himself to be more serious,
And gravitating with it to this ground,
Which, he once heard, was proper to grow wise in,
If only that so many dead lie round.

Philip Larkin, UK

Prayer

Come, let us also lift our hands,
We who do not remember the custom of prayer,
We who, except for the burning fire of love,
Do not remember any idol, any god.
Come, let us present a petition that Life, our beloved,
Will pour tomorrow's sweetness into today's poison;
That for those who have not strength for the burden of the
    days,
May it make night and day weigh light on their eyelashes;
For those whose eyes have not strength for seeing the face
    of dawn,
May it light some candle in their nights;

For those for whose steps there is no assistance of any road,
May it make some road luminous to their sight;
To those whose religion is pursuit of lying and hypocrisy,
May there come courage for denial, resolution for truth;
To those whose heads are awaiting the sword of oppression,
May there come capacity to shake off the murderer's hand.
The hidden secret of love is the fevered soul, with which
Let us today make a covenant, and let its fever be slaked;
The word of Truth, which throbs in the heart like a thorn,
Let us today accept, and the anguish be wiped out.

Faiz Ahmed Faiz, Pakistan
(translated by V. Kiernan)

Man: a definition

Describing the Man
As phenomenon
First came the saint,
Pointing up with his finger
Far beyond the stars from where
This phantom of life might have descended.

Speculating on Man
As divine manifestation
Appeared the philosopher,
Pointing down below
The surface of the sea,
Where reflection of the full moon
Had broken and scattered upon billow-breakers.

Calculating the derivation of Man
As an evolutionary pattern
Stood up the scientist,
With skulls and bones of
Primeval creatures, with helpless conviction
Demonstrating proof, proffering evidence
That one second in the annals of time
Must be equal to a thousand years, or more.

Interpreting the existence of Man
As an organising force
Emerged the sociologist,
With complicated charts and graphs
Evaluating centuries of man's achievements
In four progressive dimensions.

Finally came the poet,
Accepting Man as basically unique,
Defining in one breath,
Man is the only species who can laugh at himself.

R.P. Singh, India

Sorrow descends on me

Sorrow descends on me
with the dark:

Life is not simple
nor pleasant
nor even bearable:

and on this night
as on a thousand other nights
there are men who languish
in the dark

with whom I laughed
with whom the intolerable burden
of unfreedom
presses
like the dark

Dennis Brutus, South Africa

A patriot to patriots

Respect my silence. A head used to betrayals
is scared to show its tongue.

I have, too often, mistaken for an ocean
of voices the roar of city rain, seen too many

of what I thought men shrivel, finding holes
that would surprise them, like the rodent,

and the infinite variety of the rodent,
house-rat and field-rat, and church-mouse, and poets not meant

to acquire the profile of the mongoose,
the mongoose that sways to the curled flute of the serpent

mesmerised by old ideas of evil, until
in shriven panic the tainted foreteeth sink

in the neck to bite off an old question,
by which I mean, sir, what is evil? Men?

Such as the evil in history, the treachery of friends.
Listen, this is an old snake talking, be quiet,

do not cut me off. I have eaten and have seen it.
Respect my quiet. I have seen revolutions turn

into a barbarous, betrayed riot,
I mistook such voices for the mountain rain,

for a million tongues budding in flowers from asphalt,
spears and crystals of tongues,

believe in my bitterness, believe this venom.
I no longer list to such wrongs.

A cold head, used to betrayal,
has shown you its tongue.

Derek Walcott, West Indies

104

To those students who perished in the struggle for peace and freedom

Who are these generous ones,
Of whose blood
The gold coins, clink, clink,
Into the earth's continually thirsty
Begging-bowl are running,
Are filling up the begging-bowl?
Who are these young men, oh native land of theirs,
These spendthrifts
Of whose bodies
The brimming youth's pure gold
Is thus in fragments in the dust,
Is thus scattered street by street,
Oh their native land, oh native land?
Why did they tear out, laughing, and throw away,
These eyes their sapphires,
These lips their coral?
The restless silver of these hands,
To what use did it come, into whose possession did it fall?
Oh questioning foreigner,
These boys and youths
Are fresh pearls of that light,
Are new-grown buds of that fire,
From which sweet light and hot fire
In the dark night of tyranny there burst forth
The garden of the dawn of rebellion,
And there was dawn in every mind and body.
The silver and gold of these bodies,
The sapphire and coral of these faces,
Glittering, glittering, shining, shining —
The foreigner who wishes to see,
Let him come close and look his fill:
These are the ornament of the queen of life,
These are the bracelet of the goddess of peace.

Faiz Ahmed Faiz, Pakistan
(translated by V. Kiernan)

A Welsh testament

All right, I was Welsh. Does it matter?
I spoke the tongue that was passed on
To me in the place I happened to be,
A place huddled between grey walls
Of cloud for at least half the year.
My word for heaven was not yours.
The word for hell had a sharp edge
Put on it by the hand of the wind
Honing, honing with a shrill sound
Day and night. Nothing that Glyn Dŵr
Knew was armour against the rain's
Missiles. What was descent from him?

Even God had a Welsh name:
We spoke to him in the old language;
He was to have a peculiar care
For the Welsh people. History showed us
He was too big to be nailed to the wall
Of a stone chapel, yet still we crammed him
Between the boards of a black book.

Yet men sought us despite this.
My high cheek-bones, my length of skull
Drew them as to a rare portrait
By a dead master. I saw them stare
From their long cars, as I passed knee-deep
In ewes and wethers. I saw them stand
By the thorn hedges, watching me string
The far flocks on a shrill whistle.

And always there was their eyes' strong
Pressure on me: You are Welsh, they said;
Speak to us so; keep your fields free
Of the smell of petrol, the loud roar
Of hot tractors; we must have peace
And quietness.

Is a museum
Peace? I asked. Am I the keeper
Of the heart's relics, blowing the dust
In my own eyes? I am a man;
I never wanted the drab role
Life assigned me, an actor playing
To the past's audience upon a stage
Of earth and stone; the absurd label
Of birth, of race hanging askew
About my shoulders. I was in prison
Until you came; your voice was a key
Turning in the enormous lock
Of hopelessness. Did the door open
To let me out or yourselves in?

R.S. Thomas, UK

Africa

Africa my Africa
Africa of proud warriors in ancestral savannahs
Africa of whom my grandmother sings
On the banks of the distant river
I have never known you
But your blood flows in my veins
Your beautiful black blood that irrigates the fields
The blood of your sweat
The sweat of your work
The work of your slavery
The slavery of your children
Africa tell me Africa
Is this you this back that is bent
This back that breaks under the weight of humiliation
This back trembling with red scars
And saying yes to the whip under the midday sun
But a grave voice answers me
Impetuous son that tree young and strong
That tree there
In splendid loneliness amidst white and faded flowers
That is Africa your Africa
That grows again patiently obstinately
And its fruit gradually acquire
The bitter taste of liberty.

David Diop, Senegal
(translated by G. Moore and U. Beier)

Her brains have been eaten away
by the termites of education

Sometimes I think
Basia is mad.

She should be taken
To the witchdoctor
So he can drive off
The evil spirits
That have entered
Her head,
The evil spirits
That have changed
Her thinking.

Basia boldly declares
She wants equality;
She wants women
To be equal to men!

She is not ashamed
To say these things
In the presence of men;
She is not ashamed
To say these things
When the sun is shining brightly.

Basia says
Women must have
As much right as men
To go where they want
When they want,
To do what they want

When they want!

continued

Basia leads
A rebellious group
Of women
Who call themselves
'The Council'.
I'm told
They only discuss men
In their meetings.

They talk
Of how bad
Our customs are.
How men
Have made women
Their slaves
To carry firewood,
To cook for them,
To fetch water.

They say
The wives of the whitemen
Just sit at home
While servants
Do their work!

They ask
Why they should not
Be treated
Like the wives
Of the whitemen.

Sometimes
When Basia talks of these things
In my presence
I have pity on her.
I have the pity
Because I think
She needs help.

She needs the medicine man
To throw some bones
So as to drive off
The evil spirits
That have entered
Her head.

In my land
Women do the kitchen work,
Women look after children
And their husbands.

These are the customs
Basia and her 'Council'
Have rejected;
These are the customs
They call primitive.

The spirits that have entered
Basia's head
Are very active
When Basia meets other women.
Basia would talk and talk
Like a politician
Campaigning for votes.
She will tell them
How selfish men are,
How men will do anything
To get what they want.

*

Basia works in an office
Together with a number
Of other women.
They are always talking
About men.
Sometimes they discuss
Men's dresses;
Sometimes they talk   *continued*

111

Of men's stupidity,
Of men they have sacked,
Of men dying for them,
Of men they want.

When the machine
That tells time
Orders them out of the office,
They run off
To enter the large
Moving houses
Where men with big bellies
Wait for them.

Sometimes
I sit and wonder
Why women

Should be employed
In the offices
If they spend their time
Talking about men.

These questions
Bothered me
So much
That one day
I ventured to ask
How Basia got her job.
Basia proudly declared
She knew the necessary people.

Basia continues to speak
Of Equality
Of The Sexes!

Sometimes when I'm alone
Thoughts drift through my mind
Like clouds
Across the clear blue sky,

Thoughts of what Basia says
About The Equality of Sexes.

I sometimes think
Basia's mad ideas
Might infect me.
I had rather
Keep away
From these mad ideas.

I believe
Basia has no brains;
Her brains
Have been eaten away
By the termites
Of education,
Her brains have been invaded
By the maggots
Of the whiteman's knowledge,
Of the whiteman's customs
And of her newly acquired pride.

Basia rejects me
Because I do not
Support her mad ideas.
Basia now tells me
There are many other men
Willing to accept her new ways
And that she would find another man
Who will respect
Her views.

When she says these things
Basia pretends to be very innocent;
She pretends I am the cause
Of the volcanic eruptions
In our love,
Of the thunderstorms
In our relationship.

Joseph Buruga, East Africa

Arts, Sport and Play

from   Rites

Look wha' happen las' week at de O-
val!

At de Oval?
Wha' happen las' week at de Oval?

You mean to say that you come
in here wid dat lime-skin cone

that you callin' a hat
pun you head, an' them slip slop shoe strap

on to you foot like a touris';
you sprawl you ass

all over my chair widdout ask-
in' me please leave nor licence,

wastin' muh time when you know very well that uh cahn fine
enough to finish these zoot suits

'fore Christmas; an' on top
o' all this, you could wine up de nerve to stop

me cool cool cool in de middle
o' all me needle

an' t 'read; make me prick me hand im me haste;
an' tell me broad an' bole to me face

THAT YOU DOAN REALLY KNOW WHA' HAPPEN
At Kensington Oval?

We was *only* playin' de MCC, man;
M — C — C
who come all de way out from Inglan.

We was battin', you see;
score wasn't too bad; one
hurren an' ninety-

seven fuh three.
The openers out, Tae Worrell out,
Everton Weekes jus' glide two fuh fifty

an' jack, is de GIANT to come!
Feller name Wardle
was bowlin'; tossin' it up

sweet sweet slow-medium syrup.
Firs' ball . . .
'N . . . o . . . o . . .'

back down de wicket to Wardle.
Secon' ball . . .
'N . . . o . . . o . . .'

Back down de wicket to Wardle.
Third ball comin' up
an' we know wha' goin' happen to syrup:

Clyde back pun he back
foot an' *prax*!
is through extra cover an' four red runs all de way.

'You see dat shot?' The people was shoutin';
'Jesus Chrise, Man, wunna see dat shot?'
All over de groun' fellers shakin' hands wid each other

as if was *they* wheelin' de willow
as if was *them* had the power;
one man run out pun de field wid a red fowl cock

goin' quawk quawk quawk in 'e han';
would 'a give it to Clyde right then an' right there
if a police hadn't stop 'e!

An' in front o' where I was sittin',
one ball-headed sceptic snatch hat off he head
as if he did crazy

an' pointin' he finger at Wardle,
he jump up an' down
like a sun-shatter daisy an' bawl

117

out: 'B . . . L . . . O . . . O . . . D, B . . . I . . . G B . . . O . . . Y
bring me he B . . . L . . . O . . . O . . . D.'
Who would'a think that for twenty-

five years he was standin' up there
in them Post Office cages, lickin' gloy
pun de Gover'ment stamps.

If uh wasn't there to see fuh meself,
I would'a never believe it,
I would'a never believe it.

But I say it once an' I say it agen:
When things goin' good, you cahn touch
we; but leh murder start an' you cahn fine a man to hole up
    de side.

Like when Laker come on.
Goin' remember what happenin' then
for the rest o' me life.

This Laker a quiet tall heavy-face fellow
who before he start to do anything ser'ous
is hitch up he pants round he belly.

He bowlin' off-breaks.
Int makin' no fuss
jus' toss up de firs'

one an' *bap*!
Clyde play forward firm
an' de ball hit he pad

an' fly up over de wicket.
Boy, *dis* is cricket!
Laker shift weight

an' toss up de secon';
it pitchin' off-stump an' comin' back sharp
wid de men in de leg trap shinin' like shark.

Clyde stretchin' right out like a man in de dark
an' he kill it.
'N . . . O . . . O . . . O,' from de schoolboys, 'hit it, hit it.'

Boy, dis is *cricket.*
Then Laker come down wid he third
one. He wrap up de ball in de palm

o' he han' like a package
AN' MAKE CLYDE WALCOTT LOOK FOOLISH.
Mister man, could'a hear

all de flies that was buzzin' out there
round de bread carts; could'a hear
if de empire fart.

An' then blue murder start:
'Kill one o' dem, Clyde,' some wise-
wun was shoutin', 'knock he skull off;

doan let them tangle you up in no leg trap;
use de feet dat God give you!'
Ev'ry blabber mout' talkin',

ev'ry man jack givin' advice;
but we so frighten now at what happenin' there
we could piss we pants if we doan have a care.

'*Swing de bat, man,*' one feller was shoutin';
an' Clyde swing de bat but de bat miss
de ball an' de ball hit he pad

an' he pad went *biff*
like you beatin' bed
an' de empire han' stick

in de air
like Francis who dead
an' de bess o' we batsmen out.

The crowd so surprise you int hearin' a shout.
Ev'ry mout' loss.
But I say it once an' I say it agen:

when things goin' good, you cahn touch
we; but leh murder start
an' ol'man, you cahn fine a man to hole up de side . . . .

Edward Brathwaite, West Indies

Runner

(Commentary for a film, directed by Donald Owen and produced by the National Film Board of Canada)

First Voice
Excellence is a gift: among mankind
To one is assigned a ready wit,
To another swiftness of eye or foot.

Art which raises Nature to perfection
Itself demands the passion of the elect
Who expect to win.

As Pindar long ago in Greece was proud to hail
Thessalian Hippokleas, even so
It is meet we praise in our days fleet-footed
Bruce Kidd from Toronto.

Announcer
The Place of Training: The East York Track Club.
The Trainer: Fred Foote.
The Training Schedule: two hours a day, six days a week.
Average distance run per week: two hundred miles.

Second Voice
All visible visibly
Moving things
Spin or swing
One of the two,
Move, as the limbs
Of a runner do,
To and fro,
Forward and back,
Or, as they swiftly
Carry him,
In orbit go
Round an endless track.

120

So, everywhere, every
Creature disporting
Itself according
To the law of its making
In the rivals' dance
Of a balanced pair,
Or the ring-dance
Round a common centre
Delights the eye
By its symmetry
As it changes place,
Blessing the unchangeable
Absolute rest
Of the space all share.

First Voice
Speed is inborn in sprinter's muscle,
But long learning alone can build
Stamina and strength.

Second Voice
  By instruction only
Can limbs learn to live their movements
Without thinking.

First Voice
  All important
Is leg-action: arms are for balance.

Second Voice
Of more moment is mileage run
Than time taken.

continued

Announcer
Now for the main event of this Dominion Day Celebration in
  East York:
The Two-mile Invitation Race.

We have three international track stars here this afternoon:
Lt Max Truex of the United States Navy in the dark trunks,
Laszlo Tabori, late of Hungary in the light trunks,
And, of course,
Toronto's own Bruce Kidd.

The runners are lining up for the start mark:
The officials are ready.
They're off!

They're jockeying for position round the first bend.
Tabori's taking a strong lead.
Kidd's right after him.
Now Truex is moving out in front.
Tabori's coming up strong behind him.
Coming down the straightway now, it's
Tabori
Truex
Kidd.

First Voice
Rivals should ride to the race together,
Be firm friends.

Second Voice
    Foolish is he
Who, greedy for victory, grits his teeth,
Frowns fiercely before contests,
And no neighbour.

First Voice
    It is nice to win,
But sport shall be loved by losers also:
Foul is envy.

Second Voice
      False are those
With warm words for the winner after
A poor race.

First Voice
      Pleasing to the ear
Are clapping crowds, but the cold stop-watch
Tells the truth.

Second Voice
      There is time and place
For a fine performance: Fate forbids
Mortals to be at their best always.
God-given is the great day.

Announcer
Truex is spurting ahead,
But Tabori and Kidd are hot on his heels.
One mile to go.
The runners are maintaining a gruelling pace.

Now we have the official standing in the two-mile event.
KIDD first
TABORI second
TRUEX third.

Second Voice
The camera's eye
Does not lie,
But it cannot show
The life within,
The life of a runner,
Or yours or mine,
That race which is neither
Fast nor slow,
For nothing can ever
Happen twice,

continued

That story which moves
Like music when
Begotten notes
New notes beget,
Making the flowing
Of Time a growing,
Till what it could be
At last it is,
Where Fate is Freedom,
Grace and Surprise.

W.H. Auden, UK

New Year's morning

the children come searching
among the scattered red of the road
for unexploded crackers,
turning over the charred heaps
and eagerly picking up one or two;

the night's dews have made them damp,
they no longer sound sharply,
but even a flash and a pop
is an artistic success,
an event of power.

their small faces smile a celebration

as echoes rock the neighbourhood,
machine-gun into the new year.

Lee Tzu Pheng, Singapore

from   Report on a Caribbean festival of arts

The lissom dancers curve,
the lissom dancers carve
sharp sculptures from the air;
the rapid bodies chisel
swift arabesques and rare,
the rapid bodies whistle
like sabres keen and bare.

then the
quick quick quick
trrik trrik trrik
of the castanets
and the
synocopated thick
percussive *boom-a-lick*
-a-boom
of tambourines and cymbals,
triangles, gongs,
and big bass drums.

but what I am most enjoying,

even more than seeing actors
serious behind false whiskers
and figures contrapposto
jumping a new calypso
or even more than hearing
a caribbean philharmonia
managing a great eroica
is watching youngsters gather
in a midnight cafeteria
and quietly of mouth,
regardless of the provinces
of the nine enchanting Muses,
discuss the future territory
of imagination linked to memory;

sensing dark winds surging   *A.L. Hendriks,*
from the mountains of the south.   *West Indies*

125

Husa

I' beatin' me husa drum
all year long, an'
I ain't waitin' for no 'ficial festival;
all I want is me personal bacchanal.

Bin-bibi-din-bong!
Bibi-din-bong!

We beatin' Oil-drum,
Dus'-bin, Bamboo, Zapa-too, an'
makin' music from any ol' shoe'.

Walkin' from town to St James,
I' moverin' like I' in Olympic Games,
an 'eatin' me roti
wit' me rum in me han',
while I' lookin' for a husa band
to join.

Brother! I' jumpin' up in the husa band
in me own mind, yes, an'
even makin' 'eadstan', an'
'oldin' plenty woman roun' them waist, an'
feelin' the people' rhythm,
as I' jumpin' up
in the husa band
in me own mind.
I ain' waitin' for no 'ficial festival;
all I want is me personal bacchanal.

Bin-bibi-din-bong!
Bibi-din-bong!

I' jumpin' up
in the husa band
in me own mind.

Bin-bibi-din-bong!
Bibi-din-bong!

Frank John, West Indies

126

Limbo

And limbo stick is the silence in front of me
limbo

limbo
limbo like me
limbo
limbo like me

long dark night is the silence in front of me
limbo
limbo like me

stick hit sound
and the ship like it ready

stick hit sound
and the dark still steady

limbo
limbo like me

long dark deck and the water surrounding me
long dark deck and the silence is over me

limbo
limbo like me

stick is the whip
and the dark deck is slavery

stick is the whip
and the dark deck is slavery

limbo
limbo like me

drum stick knock
and the darkness is over me

knees spread wide
and the water is hiding me

continued

limbo
limbo like me

knees spread wide
and the dark ground is under me

down
down
down

and the drummer is calling me

limbo
limbo like me

sun coming up
and the drummers are praising me

out of the dark
and the dumb gods are raising me

up
up
up

and the music is saving me

hot
slow
step

on the burning ground.

Edward Brathwaite, West Indies

Piano and drums

When at break of day at a riverside
I hear jungle drums telegraphing
the mystic rhythm, urgent, raw
like bleeding flesh, speaking of
primal youth and the beginning,
I see the panther ready to pounce,
the leopard snarling about to leap
and the hunters crouch with spears poised;

And my blood ripples, turns torrent,
topples the years and at once I'm
in my mother's lap a suckling;
at once I'm walking simple
paths with no innovations,
rugged, fashioned with the naked
warmth of hurrying feet and groping hearts
in green leaves and wild flowers pulsing.

Then I hear a wailing piano
solo speaking of complex ways
in tear-furrowed concerto;
of far-away lands
and new horizons with
coaxing diminuendo, counterpoint,
crescendo. But lost in the labyrinth
of its complexities, it ends in the middle
of a phrase at a daggerpoint.

And I lost in the morning mist
of an age at a riverside keep
wandering in the mystic rhythm
of jungle drums and the concerto.

Gabriel Okara, Nigeria

129

Slow guitar
(from *Didn't He Ramble*)

Bring me now where the warm wind
blows, where the grasses
sigh, where the sweet
tongued blossom flowers

where the showers
fan soft like a fisherman's
net through the sweet-
ened air

Bring me now where the workers
rest, where the cotton drifts,
where the rivers are
and the minstrel sits

on the logwood stump
with the dreams of his slow guitar.

Edward Brathwaite, West Indies,

Parting of ways

Leaving behind the family's hut
where he was born and raised
and listened to his sister's chants

The village one day awoke
bestowed its pastoral pride
and bid him farewell

On his return from England
the neighbours came
flocked round him.
Oddly his first act
was to read them aloud
the opening lines of Paradise Lost
and followed this with a talk
about Longfellow
and his love of Pope

Their startled eagerness
held beyond a reading from Wordsworth
and their eyes lost a little glimmer
as he adjusted his voice
to recapture an Oxford accent

He then unfolded an album
and the village saw for the first time
a grey charm before them
the Thames as it moves silently east
past the Tower Bridge

The village listened patiently
trapped at the edge
of precise
phrasing
unique learning
and there was silence

continued

Some people rose and collected
their stools and walking sticks
parted
and moved their peasant features away
like a squatter rises
recollects himself
seeing his presence
out of harmony
with things

There was an old baobab tree
in the centre of the village
here they went and sat
to regroup back their dignity
here where they know themselves best
in the clearness
of a calm quiet
shade

Khadambi Asalache, Kenya

Poetry for supper

'Listen, now, verse should be as natural
As the small tuber that feeds on muck
And grows slowly from obtuse soil
To the white flower of imortal beauty.'

'Natural, hell! What was it Chaucer
Said once about the long toil
That goes like blood to the poem's making?
Leave it to nature and the verse sprawls,
Limp as bindweed, if it break at all
Life's iron crust. Man, you must sweat
And rhyme your guts taut, if you'd build
Your verse a ladder.'
                              'You speak as though
No sunlight ever surprised the mind
Groping on its cloudy path.'

'Sunlight's a thing that needs a window
Before it enter a dark room.
Windows don't happen.'

                    So two old poets,
Hunched at their beer in the low haze
Of an inn parlour, while the talk ran
Noisily by them, glib with prose.

R.S. Thomas, UK

At the grave of John Clare

Walking in the scythed churchyard, around the locked church,
Walking among the oaks and snails and mossed inscriptions
At first we failed to find the grave.
But a girl said, 'There he is: there is John Clare.'
And we stood, silent, by the ridged stone,
A stone of grey cheese.
There were no flowers for the dead ploughman
As the gilt clock fired off the hour,
Only the words:
A poet is born not made.

The dove-grey village lay in the Dutch landscape:
The level-crossing and the fields of wet barley,
The almshouses, the school, the Ebenezer Chapel,
The two pubs, and the signposts
To Stamford, To Maxey
From the pages of biography.
And later, sitting in the church
Among the unstuffed hassocks,
And smoking a pipe on the gate
At Maxey Crossing,
I thought of the dead poet:

Of the books and letters in the Peterborough Museum,
The huge, mad writing.
Of the way he walked, with one foot in the furrow,
Or hurried, terrified, as a child to fetch the flour from Maxey
Expecting from every turn a Caliban.
Of London, Charles Lamb and Hazlitt,
The bad grammar, the spelling, the invented words,
And the poetry bursting like a diamond bomb.
I thought of the last days, the old man
Sitting alone in the porch of All Saints' in Northampton,
And the dead poet trundling home to Helpston.

O Clare! Your poetry clear, translucent
As your lovely name,
I salute you with tears.
And, coming out on the green from the Parting Pot,
I notice a bicycle tyre
Hanging from the high stone feathers of your monument.

Charles Causley, UK

The phoenix

Black with fire a small bird tries the air
on newly-tempered wing,
impatient for the ornament of rain —

a small bird scrap-metallic,
conveying marvel and defying terms.

We have this dearth of light domestic words
to discipline, persuade to feather:
those we scrape together have no steel,
stand unequal to the flame.
In such a situation
they lack the quality of laughter,
the subtlety of flight.
Their airborne route is brief,
their transport soft and fragmentary.
They powder out between fingers.

Black with fire a small bird stabs the air,
not unaware of habit.

Amy Hollins, UK

135

Places

Mirapakayalu

In September we import
A little Indian summer.
When Surrey trees are a patchwork
Of brown and green and gold,
And the fallen leaves reflect
The dampness of the sky,
We bring into our warm bright kitchen
Fingers of flame on dark green foliage.
'Capsicum' the garden centre's label
Proclaims on the plant pot.
The sight of chillies warms the memory
Before the palate,
Until the leaves wither
And the beacons dried and powdered
Are set in the winter herb-store.

Across thousands of miles and millions of minutes
The Delta ferry plies.
The iron-rimmed wooden wheels
Of carts, and hump-backed oxen
Crowd round the jeep
And all their cargo
Is pungent sacks packed with chilli harvest.
The senses thrill to
Strange sights and sounds and smells.
The sun sinks upstream
Into the Godavari,
And rows of palm trees cast long shadows
On the kitchen floor.

Martin James, UK

A visit to Jamaica
and a walk through Kingston

My peripheral eye caught
familiar angles. I knew he hid
with the waiting people
of the city's backland.

My steps halted,
in joy in fear,
beside a bowed wreck.

It was a busily suspicious face,
something seldom aroused,
the clothes a stink nest.
My memory sharpened the jolly
stutterer at school.

My anxious voice bounced loose
like an old embrace of boyhood.
Leo, man! I said.

A glare unlidded his old
froggy eyes. A rush of memory opened
his mouth and arms. A twist
hardened a contemptuous mouth
in a knotted beard.

He slowly drew a final door.
It seemed my voice,
my dress, my look, wounded him
as if I was a foreign reporter,
to expose him, to say
he chickened out on his children.

His word staggering manhood
had linked his first girl, I knew.
He had sustained a fluency   *continued*

139

of eight new lives. I knew
he had left them, years now.

But I knew him before all that.
Leo! My voice pulled
at his hurried and ragged turn away.
My early village friend was armless
and wordless for me.

Was this the final man?
There was no joke,
no touch.

Leo! I whispered.
His shuffles mounted
a wider and wider distance.

James Berry, *West Indies*

Hotel room, 12th floor

This morning I watched from here
a helicopter skirting like a damaged insect
the Empire State Building, that
jumbo size dentist's drill, and landing
on the roof of the PanAm skyscraper.
But now midnight has come in
from foreign places. Its uncivilised darkness
is shot at by a million lit windows, all
ups and acrosses.

But midnight is not
so easily defeated. I lie in bed, between
a radio and a television set, and hear
the wildest of warwhoops continually ululating through
the glittering canyons and gulches —
police cars and ambulances racing
to the broken bones, the harsh screaming
from coldwater flats, the blood
glazed on sidewalks.

The frontier is never
somewhere else. And no stockades
can keep the midnight out.

Norman MacCaig, UK

On leaving Wantage 1972

I like the way these old brick garden walls
Unevenly run down to Letcombe Brook.
I like the mist of green about the elms .
In earliest leaf-time. More intensely green
The duck-weed undulates; a mud-grey trout
Hovers and darts away at my approach.
  From rumpled beds on far-off new estates,
From houses over shops along the square,
From red-brick villas somewhat further out,
Ringers arrive, converging on the tower.
  Third Sunday after Easter. Public ways
Reek faintly yet of last night's fish and chips.
The plumes of smoke from upright chimney-pots
Denote the death of last week's Sunday press,
While this week's waits on many a step and sill
Unopened, folded, supplements and all.
  Suddenly on the unsuspecting air
The bells clash out. It seems a miracle
That leaf and flower should never even stir
In such great waves of medieval sound:
They ripple over roofs to fields and farms
So that 'the fellowship of Christ's religion'
Is roused to breakfast, church or sleep again.
  From this wide vale, where all our married lives
We two have lived, we now are whirled away
Momently clinging to the things we knew —
Friends, footpaths, hedges, house and animals —
Till, borne along like twigs and bits of straw,
We sink below the sliding stream of time.

John Betjeman, UK

In the Huon Valley

Propped boughs are heavy with apples,
Springtime quite forgotten.
Pears ripen yellow. The wasp
Knows where windfalls lie rotten.

Juices grow rich with sun.
These autumn days are still:
The glassy river reflects
Elm-gold up the hill,

And big white plumes of rushes.
Life is full of returns;
It isn't true that one never
Profits, never learns:

Something is gathered in,
Worth the lifting and stacking;
Apples roll through the graders,
The sheds are noisy with packing.

James McAuley, Australia

God rest ye merry gentlemen

Splitting from Jack Delaney's, Sheridan Square,
that winter night, stewed, seasoned in bourbon,
my body kindled by the whistling air
snowing the Village that Christ was reborn,
I lurched like any lush by his own glow
across towards Sixth, and froze before the tracks
of footprints bleeding on the virgin snow.
I tracked them where they led across the street
to the bright side, entering the wax-
sealed smell of neon, human heat,
some all-night diner with its wise-guy cook
his stub thumb in my bowl of stew and one
man's pulped and beaten face, its look
acknowledging all that, white-dark outside,
was possible: some beast prowling the block,
something fur-clotted, running wild
beyond the boundary of will. Outside,
more snow had fallen. My heart charred.
I longed for darkness, evil that was warm.
Walking, I'd stop and turn. What had I heard,
wheezing behind my heel with whitening breath?
Nothing. Sixth Avenue yawned wet and wide.
The night was white. There was nowhere to hide.

Derek Walcott, West Indies

The Welsh hill country

Too far for you to see
The fluke and the foot-rot and the fat maggot
Gnawing the skin from the small bones,
The sheep are grazing at Bwlch-y-Fedwen,
Arranged romantically in the usual manner
On a bleak background of bald stone.

Too far for you to see
The moss and the mould on the cold chimneys,
The nettles growing through the cracked doors,
The houses stand empty at Nant-yr-Eira,
There are holes in the roofs that are thatched with sunlight,
And the fields are reverting to the bare moor.

Too far, too far to see
The set of his eyes and the slow phthisis
Wasting his frame under the ripped coat,
There's a man still farming at Ty'n-y-Fawnog,
Contributing grimly to the accepted pattern,
The embryo music dead in his throat.

R.S. Thomas, UK

Ibadan

Ibadan,
      running splash of rust
and gold — flung and scattered
among seven hills like broken
china in the sun

J.P. Clark, Nigeria

145

A sojourn in Jhalda

Here I see people more clearly,
one by one.
Their hands,
one before, one after,
give love or hate
like a lump of earth.

In the clean silence
of trees, clouds
and the sun,
their words, like small saplings,
offer beauty.

Their sensuousness
shines — their women
with picked bosom
and half-hid thighs.

These people are birds.
With their method
of labour, there is
the loveliness of wings.

Here I am —
like a boat with sails.
So much air,
so much love to live with.

Subhas Chandra Saha, India

Epiphany I

(from the 'Tower' Class Room at St George's College, Jamaica,
during target practice from shore to sea)

I have lifted my eyes above their heads
    And looked across the green protecting arm
    That dams and breaks atlantic dreads;
From class-room tower and our babel to calm
    Of inner sea unruffled by the slightest foam,
    To open sea's roughcast and blue-white charm.

The heard and unseen arc of the shell strikes home
    The Moses staff causing from the sea to sprout
    A court-yard fountain, if heaven be the dome
Of blue upon the salt blue drought
    Of desert ocean that needed this white rose,
    This cluster white of bamboo shoots that out
Of blue rock at the strike of Moses grows
    And pauses at the balance point that makes
    The shape, that holds the pattern's close.

The bamboo plumes outward, white and takes
    Its shape forever rooted in this sleeping sea
    The hurrying motion of innumerable flakes
Of white and blue from ocean's rock I see
    As motionless and full, unhurried calm,
    As balanced as permanent as a perfect tree.

I look back at their faces' slight alarm
    And wide-eyed wonder at my wandering —
    These children's balanced being to be the palm
That bends to every wind's imposturing!
    Each searching eye is a murky pool
    Slowly lighted by shafts of quivering
Laughter. We turn the pages and make the best of school.

John Figueroa,
West Indies

from *Under another sky*

Through holes in a wall, as it were,
lamps burned in the fog,
in a basement flat, conversation
filled the night, while Ravi Shankor,
cigarette stubs, empty bottles of stout
and crisps provided the necessary pauses.
He had spent his youth whoring
after English gods.

There is something to be said for exile:
you learn roots are deep. That language
is a tree, loses colour
under another sky. The bark
disappears with the snow
and branches become hoarse.
However, the most reassuring thing
about the past is that it happened.

Dressed in tweeds or grey flannel,
in suburban pockets
bursting with immigrants —
'coloureds' is what they call us
over there — the city is no jewel, either.
But ugly and wet.
Lanes, full of smoke and litter,
with puddles of unwashed English children.

On New Year's Eve he heard an old man
at Trafalgar Square: It's no use
trying to change people. They'll be
what they are. An Empire's
last words are heard on the hot sands
of Africa. The da Gamas, Clives, Dupleixs
are back. Victoria sleeps on her island alone,
an old hag, shaking her invincible locks.

Standing on Westminster Bridge it seemed
the Thames had clogged the chariot wheels
of Boadicea to a stone. Under the shadow
of poplars the river divides
the city from the night. The noises
reappear, of early trains, the milkman,
and the events of the day become
vocal in the newsboy.

R. Parthasarathy, India

The place where I've not been

The place where I have not been
I never shall be.
The place where I have been
Is as though I have never been there. People stray
Far from the places where they were born
And far from the words which were spoken
As if by their mouths
And still wide of the promise
Which they were promised.

And they eat standing and die sitting
And lying down they remember.
And what I shall never in the world return to
And look at, I am to love for ever.
Only a stranger will return to my place. But I will set down
All these things once more, as Moses did,

After he smashed the first tablets.

Yehuda Amichai, Israel
(translated by Assia Gutman)

Glossary

Our people

The song of the banana man
janga: a crayfish found in some rivers of Jamaica.
Gros Michel and Lacatan: two varieties of banana.

Goodbye party for Miss Pushpa T.S.
bonnvoage: bon voyage: (have a) good journey.

Love

Jarri's love song
gunya: an Australian aboriginal's hut.
waddy: a native wooden war-club.
woomera: a throw-stick.
goreen: a heavy throw-stick used in hunting.
pitcheri, or *pituri:* a native plant chewed by some tribes
    for its narcotic properties.
two tails: little gecko lizards shed the tail when seized;
    it grows again, but often with abnormalities, so that double
    tails are to be seen.

Life and death

Requiem for a Caribbean fisherman
braata: something extra, given to a good customer.

Animals

We all have our superstitions
shrawan: one of the rainy monsoon months, e.g. July.
Shreshnag: The God Shiva, one of the Hindu triad of gods,
    rides on Shreshnag, a sort of serpent.

151

Nature and seasons

Hurricane
jump-poco: to dance with the jigging motion characteristic
   of the local, traditional dancing.
chew-stick: chaw-stick; a common creeper in the West
   Indies, with thin, flexible stems chewed as an agreeable
   medicine good for the stomach. A chaw-stick can also be
   kept, with frayed-out ends, to clean the teeth.

Myth . . . legend . . . the past

Skirmish at Maldon
byrnies: breastplates.

Arts, sport and play

Report on a Caribbean festival of arts
contrapposto: in painting and sculpture, this refers to
   the crossing of limbs and contrasting of masses. Here,
   the poet may simply mean that the dancers are facing their
   partners.
eroica: Beethoven's Eroica Symphony.

Husa
husa drum: more commonly known by the Creole spelling,
   hoosay drum; this is a drum used by the West Indian comm-
   unity for their Hoosay (or Husain) festival.
Zapa-too: the Zapa-too is played in a Tamboo bamboo band.
   It consists of two pieces of bamboo which are beaten
   together. The Tamboo bamboo band was a precursor
   of the steel band.
roti: a form of Paratha, as used in Indian cuisine, usually
   eaten, like bread, with something else.

Limbo
limbo: a West Indian dance in which the dancer bends backwards, passing — without touching — under a bar, which is progressively lowered.

Places

Mirapakayalu
Mirapakayalu: chilli.

Acknowledgements

For permission to reproduce copyright material the editors and publisher are grateful to the following:

Our People

Oxford University Press (Pakistan) for 'I am glad to be up and about' from *First Voices: Six Poets from Pakistan*

Evan Jones and Southbend Investments S.A. and Evans Brothers Ltd for 'The song of the banana man' from *Caribbean Voices*

Mrs J. Baxter and Oxford University Press (New Zealand) for 'Lament for Barney Flanagan' from *The Rock Woman*

Wole Soyinka and African Universities Press for 'Telephone conversation' from *Reflections*

United Writers for 'The old man of Birmingham' from *The Voice of the Indian Poets*

George Allen & Unwin (Publishers) Ltd for 'Goodbye party for Miss Pushpa T.S.' from *The Shell and the Rain*

Workshop Press for 'Neighbour, tenth floor' from *Madonna of the Unknown Nation*

New Poetry, Workshop Press for 'Offal'

Skylark Publications for 'Beggars' from *Effusion*

New Poetry, Workshop Press for 'The experiment'

Heinemann Educational Books Ltd for 'Riot area' from *Young Commonwealth Poets '65*

Kwesi Brew and Evans Brothers Ltd for 'Wooden dolls and dreams' from *African Voices*

Writers Workshop for 'The little chapel' from *Cyclone in Pakistan*

Roger McGough and Hope Leresche & Sayle for 'My busconductor' © 1967, from *The Mersey Sound*, Penguin Modern Poets 10

Rosemary Joseph and Oxford University Press for 'Baking day' from *A Group Anthology*

S.A. Ashraf and Venture Publications, for 'Kitchens' from *The New Harmony*

Love

George Allen & Unwin (Publishers) Ltd for 'Song for last year's wife' from *Little Johnny's Confession*

Jacaranda Press for 'Jarri's love song' from *The Dawn is at Hand*

A.P. Watt & Son and Cassell & Co. Ltd for 'A slice of wedding cake' from *Collected Poems, 1959*

Shiv K. Kumar and Writers Workshop for 'Before the beginning' from *Articulated Silences*

Heinemann Educational Books Ltd for 'The marriage of black and white' from *Poems from East Africa*

George Allen & Unwin (Publishers) Ltd for four songs from *Love Songs of Chandidas*

Heinemann Educational Books Ltd for 'The beloved' from *Poems from East Africa*

Zavallis Press and "MAM" for 'Even a bishop' from *An Anthology of Cypriot Poetry*

K. Das for 'An apology to Goutama' from *Summer in Calcutta*

John Farquharson Ltd and Constable & Co. Ltd for 'Song of the wagondriver' from *Poems*

Jon Silkin and Chatto & Windus Ltd for 'Caring for animals' from *The Peaceable Kingdom*

Amy Hollins for 'To an outstanding failure'

Life and Death

Eothen Books for 'The birth of Shaka' from *Sunset in Naivasha*

James MacGibbon and Allen Lane for 'Not waving but drowning' from *The Collected Poems of Stevie Smith*

John Farquharson Ltd and Constable & Co. Ltd for 'A country death' from *Poems*

Workshop Press for 'Requiem for a Caribbean fisherman' from *Madonna of the Unknown Nation*

Faber and Faber Ltd for 'To the Indians who died in Africa' from *Collected Poems 1909-1962*

Heinemann Educational Books Ltd for 'An un-African breakfast' from *Beneath the Jazz and Brass*

Estate of William Plomer and Jonathan Cape Ltd for 'Another old man' from *Celebrations*

Peter Owen, London for 'Life' from *Later Poems of Rabindranath Tagore*

Taner Baybars and Evans Brothers Ltd for 'Do the dying cry?' from *New Voices of the Commonwealth*

John Betjeman and John Murray (Publishers) Ltd for 'Fruit' from *A Nip in the Air*

Animals

Oxford & IBH Publishing Co. for 'We all have our superstitions' from *Indian Poetry in English, 1947-1972*

Oxford University Press for 'Army ants' from *Relations*

McClelland and Stewart Ltd, Toronto for 'Peacock' from *The Pole-Vaulter*

Faber and Faber Ltd for 'Turkeys observed' from *Death of a Naturalist*

Andrew Salkey and Evans Brothers Ltd for 'The world of the wash basin spider' from *Caribbean Voices II*

Oxford University Press for 'Keep off the grass' from *Sounds of a Cowhide Drum*

Hogarth Press Ltd for 'Feeding ducks' from *A Common Grace*

Writers Workshop for 'The hunt' from *The Hunt and Other Poems*

David Higham Associates Ltd and Macmillan & Co. Ltd for 'I saw a jolly Hunter' from *Collected Poems 1951-1975*

Norman Hidden for 'Dichloro-diphenyl-trichloro-ethane'

Nature and Seasons

H.D. Carberry and Evans brothers Ltd for 'Nature' from
Caribbean Voices

Robert Greig and Bateleur Press for 'Watermelon breakfast'
from *Bateleur Poets*

Barbara Ferland and Evans brothers Ltd for 'Hibiscus' from
Caribbean Voices

P. Lal and Writers Workshop for 'Poinsettias' from *Yakshi
from Didarganj*

Educational Publications Bureau, Singapore for 'Rain' from
The Flowering Tree

Andrew Salkey and Hutchinson Publishing Group Ltd for
extract from 'Hurricane' from *Jamaica*

Myth . . . Legend . . . The Past

Edward Lowbury and Chatto & Windus Ltd for 'The hunts-
man' from *Time for Sale*

Wole Soyinka and Martin Secker & Warburg for 'The Fulani
creation story' from *Poems of Black Africa*

Oxford University Press (Pakistan) for 'A speculation' from
First Voices: Six Poets from Pakistan

Kwesi Brew and Longman Group Ltd for 'Ancestral faces'
from *The Shadows of Laughter*

New Beacon Books Ltd for 'The pond' from *The Pond*

Heinemann Educational Books Ltd for 'Three songs of war'
from *Horn of my Love*

Norman Hidden for 'Skirmish at Maldon'

Beliefs

United Writers for 'There is one God' from *Saint Poets of
India*

Oxford University Press (Pakistan) for 'Getting to know fish'
from *First Voices: Six Poets from Pakistan*

Chaim Lewis and Juta & Co. Ltd for 'Stones' from *Shadow in the Sun*

Peter Owen Ltd for 'Worship of the Buddha' from *Later Poems of Rabindranath Tagore*

Marvell Press, England for 'Church going' from *The Less Deceived*

George Allen & Unwin (Publishers) Ltd for 'Prayer' from *Poems by Faiz*

Beach Grove Books Inc., Canada for 'Man: a definition' from *So There I Stand*

British Council of Churches for 'Sorrow descends on me' from *Other Voices, Other Places*

Derek Walcott and Jonathan Cape Ltd for 'A patriot to patriots' from *New Writing in the Caribbean*

George Allen Unwin (publishers) Ltd for 'To those students who perished in the struggle for peace and freedom' from *Poems by Faiz*

Rupert Hart-Davis Ltd/Granada Publishing Ltd for 'A Welsh testament' from *Poetry for Supper*

Penguin Books Ltd for 'Africa' from *Modern Poetry from Africa* (Penguin African Library, 1963), pp. 63-4, © Gerald Moore and Ulli Beier, 1963

East African Publishing House for 'Her brains have been eaten away by the termites of education' from *The Abondoned Hut*

Arts, Sport and Play

Oxford University Press for excerpt from 'Rites' from *Islands*

Faber & Faber Ltd for 'Runner' from *City Without Walls*

Educational Publications Bureau, Singapore for 'New Year's morning' from *The Flowering Tree*

Workshop Press for extract from 'Report on a Caribbean festival of arts' from *Madonna of the Unknown Nation*

Longman Caribbean for 'Husa' from *West Indian Poetry*

Oxford University Press for 'Limbo'

Gabriel Okara and Penguin Books Ltd for 'Piano and Drums' from *Black Orpheus* (Modern Poetry from Africa, 1963)

Oxford University Press for 'Slow Guitar' from *Rights of Passage* © Oxford University Press 1967

Eothen Books for 'Parting of ways' from *Sunset in Naivasha*

Rupert Hart-Davis Ltd/Granada Publishing Ltd for 'Poetry for supper' from *Poetry for Supper*

David Higham Associates Ltd and Macmillan Publishers Ltd for 'At the grave of John Clare' from *Collected Poems 1951-1975*

Amy Hollins for 'The Phoenix'

Places

Workshop Press for 'Mirapakayalu' from *From the Ears of the Stars*

James Berry for 'A visit to Jamaica, and a walk through Kingston'

Hogarth Press Ltd for 'Hotel room, 12th floor' from *Rings on a Tree*

John Murray (Publishers) Ltd for 'On leaving Wantage 1972' from *A Nip in the Air*

Angus & Robertson Publishers Sydney for 'In the Huon Valley' from *Collected Poems 1936-1970*

Derek Walcott and Evans Brothers Ltd for 'God rest ye merry gentlemen' from *Caribbean Voices*

Rupert Hart-Davis Ltd/Granada Publishing Ltd for 'The Welsh hill country' from *Song at the Year's Turning*

J.P. Clark and Longman Group Ltd for 'Ibadan' from *A Reed in the Tide*

S.C. Saha and Writers Workshop for 'A sojourn in Jhalda' from *Down in the Silent Night Road*

John Figueroa and Evans Brothers Ltd for 'Epiphany I' from *Caribbean Voices II*

Oxford & IBH Publishing Co. for extract from 'Under another sky' from *Indian Poetry in English*

Cape Goliard Press for 'The place where I've not been' from *Selected Poems*